MENDED
BY THE MASTER

Mended

BY THE

MASTER

PRISCELLA LEWIS

XULON PRESS ELITE

Xulon Press Elite
2301 Lucien Way #415
Maitland, FL 32751
407.339.4217
www.xulonpress.com

Paperback ISBN-13: 978-1-6628-1121-0

Ebook ISBN-13: 978-1-6628-1122-7

A book of stories and poems telling the testimony of a woman whose life was changed by God. Go through the journey of rejection, failure, mistakes, fear, love, hope and change as you read day by day, a glimpse of a life Mended by the Master.

For Bob... devoted, trustworthy and true husband of mine who understands me enough to allow me space to create. His consistent love for me has nurtured and sustained me and his actions have echoed the call to men to love their wives as Christ loves the church. In many ways he has given himself up for me. For almost 30 years he has been a constant and steadying influence in my life.

Table of Contents

Foreword

PRISCELLA LEWIS TAKES READERS ON A journey of healing and wholeness in the broken world in which we live. This is Priscella's story precisely because it is her story. Beautifully and honestly written, this book guides the reader to find the voice of God in the common events of everyday life, in our suffering and in the Scriptures that fill its pages.

I have been blessed by excerpts of the story God has written in Priscella's life for quite sometime now and the vision she has to see the hand of God everywhere. Priscella is a treasure filled with deep spiritual insight and I am grateful that others will be able to take hold of these gems she has found. Allow her story, this story, to guide yours and hear the voice of God calling to you, so you also may be Mended By The Master,

Pastor Scott Hindel,
Community Bible Church,
Rootstown, Ohio

Introduction

ALL WE REALLY HAVE IS OUR HISTORY. Folded into its seams are our hopes and our pain, our minute joys and our immense sorrows. Our lives bleed into its fabric and there, stains marks us for eternity and mar us for moments.

Stains have a certain resilience. We scrub them incessantly and like an itch that won't be satiated, they stubbornly remain. We scrub at them until our knuckles throb with the effort.

To the world, the fabric may appear spotless and unbothered, yet we recall their tainted imprint and recoil from its impact on our souls.

Our wounds weaken and wear; our stains sustain and contain us. They hold us together yet rip us apart. We hide behind the veil of our efforts to mend our lives, yet our attempts to restore ourselves somehow result in burying more deeply those secrets that enslave us.

We think our secrets are safe but they are revealed in our efforts to hide. But there is no unknown scar, stain, or blemish that is hidden from God. When he tore the veil in the temple he tore open the veil that holds our hearts captive and kept us from his great love that mends all scars, repairing the fabric of our lives and making us whole.

There is no other stain remover known to man like Jesus, the sustainer of our souls. He alone is the master-mender, the One who holds our fallen lives and presents us faultless. He is bringing to naught our efforts/repair and restore our lives. These writings reflect my efforts to repair my torn and stained life and hopefully reveal his great love through which my restoration is being wrought.

Isaiah 1:18- Come now, let us reason together, says the Lord: though your sins be as scarlet, they shall be as white as snow; though they be red like crimson, they shall be as wool.

Day 1
Healing Deep Wounds

I REALLY HAD TO GO. WHEN A FOUR-year-old child must go, well, you stop what you're doing and take care of business. Let me tell you, going to the bathroom was business, risky business, in a house occupied by ten individuals ages six months to 35 years old. Especially when one of those thirty-somethings was a man with a mean-spirited temperament. I tell you, that man had a real vicious streak. When he entered a room, we kind of just cleared out to make room for his temper. That unwritten law was laid like rubber on a hot highway across the minds of any of the eight children who could think things through.

That day, I had to go. I must not have been thinking clearly because I no sooner swung that door open and there he was, sitting on the business end of the toilet. I guess that would be enough to make someone normal a bit embarrassed to be caught in the very act. That day, nothing felt normal anymore as fear invaded me in the same kind of way that pain overtakes you when you are dumb enough to try to take something out of a hot oven without a potholder.

This was a dangerous predicament, kind of like stumbling across a rattler and he is ready to strike. Sometimes you cannot get away fast enough, or maybe you're just too young to see nothing but a beautiful fat snake with its head up. They say fear paralyzes you like a scary dream where you open your mouth to scream and just hot air comes out or you're trying to run and no matter how fast your feet move, you just stay stuck or if you're lucky enough you wake up in a cold sweat.

Let's just say I didn't have to go to the bathroom anymore by the time that snake was ready to strike. This was not going to end well. I was scared to death. My white face met eyes that were so full of lava, all you could see was the fiery black flame. They also say that the eyes of a shark are endless and seem to have no expression. That's what those eyes were like, dead with rage and they zeroed in on me.

When you are four, you have not learned how to really stretch out and run out of harm's way. So, like the child I was, fear brough me to my knees. As I went down, my body hit something hard. I got a work boot to the stomach and then the red kitchen linoleum slid under me like sliding down a hill on a snowy day.

Something was wrong with me. I could not breathe. Try hard as I could, breath would not come. The air that was kicked out of me would not come back. Can a four-year-old really understand the fear of dying? Or does trying so hard to stay alive beat out that kind of fear? It was hard to tell what went through my mind just then. When I cried for my mommy, I must have known I would live and all I wanted was a way from the mouth of the volcano and to get me some love to cover hurt. I heard the command. No, really, it was an order. "Don't touch her, she's been bad." Bad? I was too bad to be helped.

I did all I could think of to help that bad little girl. How can a four-year-old child help? I crawled as hard as I could to escape under the kitchen table. There I sat in a heap, soaked from head to toe by now in wet clothes. Wet with more than just urine, also tears and nose drippings. Why is it that when you cry really hard, your nose runs like a faucet?

Well, I stayed back under that table for a good while. Years really, until Jesus showed me how to go back and get her. The day he showed me, he held me and her and said I was his beloved. It took me a while to believe him, to really believe him. Then he healed me. How can I thank him for the healing of the broken child and creating within her a strong woman? Healing unites you with parts of yourself that pain kept from you. That is what makes you whole. I celebrate that child and I thank Jesus for work he performed on my behalf. Because of him, I am becoming new. I invite you to also become whole and allow Jesus to love and heal you.

> *Jeremiah 30:17- For I will restore health to you and your wounds I will heal, declares the Lord...*

Day 2
Help, I've fallen, and I Can't Get Up

Mark 9:22-24- And it has often cast him into fire and into water, to destroy him. But if you can do anything, have compassion on us and help us." And Jesus said to him, "If you can! All things are possible for one who believes." Immediately the father of the child cried out and said, "I believe; help my unbelief!"

HOW OFTEN WE MUSE ABOUT THE OLD commercials, the one for Verizon, "Can you hear me now?" or for Budweiser, "This one's for you." These and other slogans join the vernacular of our casual conversations. In the natural light these popular slogans are used in a somewhat humorous vein. But really, looked at from a more spiritual light, they deserve to be taken more seriously. Just think about how fallen we really are and how we cannot seem to get up. Think of how hard of hearing we can be and how we can't quite seem to muster enough faith to know for certain that Jesus is the one for us.

I came across a reading in "Our Daily Bread" where the following question was posed by author Kirsten Holmberg. She said, "When we find ourselves flattened on the cold ice of life's hardships, is there a helping hand nearby?" I paused and pondered this question. I thought of times I have been chilled to the bone and scared because no help was in sight. Sometimes we just cannot go it alone. We need someone bigger than ourselves to upright us, to help us get a steady footing.

In the gospels, Mark describes a man with a son born with a mute spirit. The father was alone and in his despair over his son who was often tormented by a spirit. Caught in the icy grip of helplessness, he cries out to Jesus, "If you can do anything, have compassion on us and help us." Jesus said to him, "If you can believe, all things are possible to him who believes." Immediately the child's father cried out with tears, "Lord I believe, help my unbelief." Jesus helped him. He rebukes the unclean spirit and took the child by the hand and lifted him up and the child arose.

Consider how Jesus takes us by the hand and lifts us up. He alone allows us to rise. He lifts us up from the icy grip of despair. He is ever our helping hand and all things are possible through him. We are often in the same set of circumstances as the woman caught in adultery, full of shame and fear over our sin. Oh, it may not be adultery, but we are on the hard ground flattened out by our utter help-lessness over something we said or did or hear. We are paralyzed by the whispers around us and fall into the black hole of hopelessness. That is when we need to reach out to the Savior. As he took that child's hand, he will take yours and lift you up.

Sometimes we need an earnest prayer, "God help my unbelief." We need to hear the Spirit calling to us, rising above the whispers in our mind. That still small voice will help you be still and know that Jesus will reach down to take your hand. You can rise in his strength and be more than your circumstances seem to allow.

Maybe you've gotten tripped up by news of a medical condition; regret from a long-ago mistake; or a habit you can't shake. Believe there is more that God has in store for you. If you are willing, God can lift you up. He stretched out His hand for the leper and He will do the same for you. He is waiting to hear you call and I believe He can hear you now.

Day 3
Torn to Shreds

*Proverbs 13:12- Hope deferred makes the heart sick
but a desire fulfilled is a tree of life.*

IN 1907, A MAN BY THE NAME OF ABBOT Augustus Low invented the first paper shredder. His vision was to offer a more compact way of disposing paper waste. Little did he know that his invention would lead to an explosion by 2020, where a world of cybersecurity would lead to procurement of paper shredders in virtually every American home. There are hundreds, if not thousands of choices to make when in the market for a paper shredder. One of the most highly recommended products features a cross cutting technique involving both horizontal and vertical cuts resulting in tiny confetti-like pieces literally torn to shreds.

Ever feel like that paper-torn to shreds by criticisms, condemnations, or accusations? I have. My father was one of the masters of how to rupture the heart and hope of a child.

When the winds of time ran through my shredded heart, I lived a scattered life that found me grasping onto anything or anyone that could bring the pieces back together again. Fulfilling the desires of the flesh consumed me all the while I searched for answers I could never find.

Behind my shadow of a life, God was at work slowly weaving and transferring healing into my soul. For despite my self-condemnation, I was to learn that He is a God of selfless, steadfast love, who, though He hated my sin thoroughly, loved me. in various ways and various times he brought people and circumstances into my life that would begin to bring hope into my sick heart.

It was the breath of the Spirit that brought together the blown away pieces of my heart. It was the very sacrifice of Jesus Christ that saved me from my sin. It was the resurrection of Jesus from the grave that called me from my self-centered tomb. It was the vast forgiveness of the Father that beckoned me too, to forgive.

My desire now is that I may know him (Philippians 3:10) and when desire comes It is a tree of life (Proverbs 13:12b) If you are feeling torn, turn to God. I assure you that he ever lives to bring healing to your broken heart.

$\mathcal{D}$ay 4
Dream to Repentance

Proverbs 14:1- The wise woman builds her house, but with her own hands the foolish one tears hers down

P ROVERBS SAYS, "THE WISE WOMAN builds her house; the foolish woman tears it down." This verse rings in my ears as I recall the dream I had last night. It was a dream where everything I touched fell apart literally and was reduced to ashes, then was carried away in a breath. When I tried to shut the door, it crumbled so there was no way to lock the door from the fear outside. It came inside to live in me. Then I began to disappear little by terror stricken little. I began to be reduced. When I was almost gone, I woke up and was in a state of not being able to discern which reality I was in. I was immensely grateful to gradually remember I was in bed in a house provided by my God-given husband. I was safe and had not disappeared into thin air. This realization brought relief and repentance. You see, I was a woman who was tearing down her house before I met the Lord. I was the epitome of someone bent toward sin and self-destruction.

Maybe we need to be reminded of where we came from to truly value the treasure we have in our lives. Maybe these kinds of dreams are needful for us to be thankful for the forgiveness Jesus gives and the power of forgiveness to transform our lives.

Although I would not want to experience that dream again, I am thankful for the pain and the fear because I feel I can be more grateful for my many blessings. I can embrace God more fully because last night I had a dream that showed me in a powerful way, just how much I have been forgiven for the sorrow and suffering my sin cost my Savior. I am so grateful for Jesus.

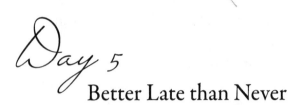

Day 5
Better Late than Never

*Isaiah 55:6- Seek the L*ORD *while he may be found; call on him while he is near.*

I WISHED A FRIEND A BELATED HAPPY birthday and added, "better late than never." As soon as I wrote those words I paused and wondered, "Is it really better late than never?"

We say that in a somewhat humorous way but when it comes to salvation there is nothing funny about it. I used to think I could put off coming to Jesus and I did until over half my life had passed over the treacherous road of sin and total neglect of what I know now is righteous.

Even then, in halfhearted commitment, I went to church and studied the Bible. There is no doubt Jesus was standing at the door knocking and though I opened the door, I kept my foot in it preventing the full light of the gospel to embrace me. Though I had moments on the mountains, I was still pursuing other gods. So many times, I missed the glory of God. There is truth in Psalm 16 when it says the sorrows of those who run after other gods shall be multiplied.

I can tell you that it is never too late to surrender to Jesus. Even the thief on the cross waited until the last minute to believe. I urge you to understand that there is no time like the present to commit your life to Him..

The joy and contentment of living a life for Jesus is unsurpassed. Come to him while he may be found, call upon Him while He is near.

I finally gave Jesus my whole heart and I can say my heart is glad. I rest in hope and I am compelled to ask you to give your all to Jesus.

Then the people rejoiced because
they had given freely with a whole heart.
1 Chronicles 29:9

Day 6
Saved by Faith

Mark 5:29- Immediately her bleeding stopped and she felt in her body that she was freed from her suffering.

S HE HAD SOMETHING ABOUT HER THAT made the people of the small-town steer clear of her. People said she was beyond repair, that she had tried for years to take care of her problems but kept reaching dead ends.

Those dead ends were not unlike her lonely life with a series of rejections of her presence and whispered conversations about her condition. Rumors were what followed her every step. After twelve years and wasting an abundance of resources, she had run out of hope and it felt like she was out of time.

Oh, she had tried. She had gone to doctors, healers, anyone who promised of a cure would possibly pan out for her. The little money she had garnered before her mysterious illness was gone. She had come up empty on every front.

If she dared to leave the one-room house where she lived, she would be shunned. People she knew her whole life would turn away from her. Crowds would part if she had the courage to enter one. Though her story was well known, spoken of three separate times in the Bible, she remains name-less. Like the fears and anxieties that hover over us, those worries without words that are low lying radar, ready to leave us speechless.

Only this morning she had heard that the true healer had come to Capernaum and she was void of all resources but one, she had a flicker of faith.

That day she had a plan that propriety would not deter. She would go out into the crowds and suffer the shame of being exposed to the rejection. Surely the kind Jesus would not reject her. She clung to this sliver of hope.

She crawled on her hands and knees close to the place she saw Him. If she could only touch the hem of His garment, she would finally be clean of the issue of blood that plagued these many years. Surely her concealed posture would not reveal her intent to touch Him. She crawled closer and stretching out her hand, she ever so slightly touched his outer garment. "Immediately the fountain of her blood was dried up and she felt in her body that she was healed of her affliction." (Mark 5:29) Jesus stopped and turning around he asked, "who touched me?" Fearing the worst, He turned in her direction and stretched out His hand. This was a gesture she had not known for all these years. He was not rejecting her; he was completing His healing. He knew her story and it was evident in the all-knowing eyes. He said to her, "Daughter, go thy way, thy faith has made you well."

From that instant, her life was altered. She had touched the Son and was forever changed and eternally cleansed. That sliver of hope had swallowed all shame and fanned into a flame a small flicker of faith.

Our lives can be transformed when we reach out to touch the Son. Do you have the courage to reach out to Him now?

Day 7
Thanksgiving

For the moments of fear
When you have been my refuge
I am thankful

For times of peace when
Your love has been steadfast
I am thankful

For the blessings of friends
Who You have given me
I am thankful

For times of uncertainty when
Jesus has anchored my hope
I am thankful

For times when You carried me
When I was too weary to walk
I am thankful

For what strength is left in my hands
That you have directed for good
I am thankful

For the breath that I breathe
And the life you breathe into me
I am thankful

For You Lord who have not forsaken
Those who seek you
I am thankful

Day 8
When I Grow Up

SOMETIMES IT TAKES A LITTLE MORE time for an abused child to grow up. It seems like it took me an inordinate amount of time to grow out of the trauma this little girl experienced. The beatings, the nightmares, the rapes, the incest, the labels put on me and the constant screaming of a mother as she was being beaten, caused deep wounds that haunt my dreams still. I awake half expecting to be yanked across the floor by my hair. Sometimes I still startle awake covered in fear.

I heard one time that hatred corrodes the container that holds it. My container, my mind my body was corroded by the acidity of the hatred spewed upon me by my father. It was leaking my very life out all along the way. For, you see, the hatred poured into a child becomes the hatred she feels for herself. I believed the lies, "you'll never amount to anything, you're ugly, you're a liar, you're worthless," and on and on went the saw blades that cut my heart to shreds.

When you try to live on the outside of hell on earth, you carry the heavy load of guilt and remorse with you. Oh, I got good at carrying that load. I got good at alleviating the burden at least seemingly with drugs and alcohol and falling into one empty relationship after another. You get good at living with pieces of yourself spread thin and stretched to the breaking point. Until one day you break, and you're faced with living in the gutter you have been wallowing in. Or you finally swallow all the pills in the bottle and fulfill the "I wish I was dead" statement you have carried inside all these years. But by some miracle you survive and continue to live the nightmare day after day.

What do you do? Where do you go when you hit the bottom of the barrel and you are too tired to fight your way back?

In my case, a husband and wife named Mary and Clark invited me to a little church in Stow, Ohio. I don't remember the music, the worship, the people around me, but I remember one thing, the sermon. It focused on Peter's sin of betraying Christ by denying he knew him. When the truth of his betrayal hit him and the rooster was crowing and Peter's eyes met the eyes of Christ, instantly Peter was gripped in the vice of guilt and shame and ran out of the courtyard and wept bitterly. Instantaneously I felt that bitter remorse over the many times I had denied that I knew Christ by my actions.

I began to realize the stark reality of sin in my life. I began to read a long-ignored Bible that had been an unused gift. At that time, in 1989 I was an unwed mother, proud of my circumstances and I had seen people dedicated their children to the Lord and I asked if I could do the same.

A team of three people came to my house to talk with me about Jesus. That night while my two-year-old sat quietly and played, I realized that I was a sinner in need of the saving grace of Jesus and I prayed. I asked Jesus to accept me as one of His children. Christ became real to me that night. For the first time I understood it was for my sin he suffered, and it was by His grace that my wounded heart could be mended. The pieces of my scattered, scarred heart could be woven back together.

No one changes over night but rather they change through the Spirit over time. It takes time for a shredded heart to trust that pieces of their broken lives can become something beautiful.

I began growing up at the age of 41 and now, thirty years later, I realize I am still becoming the woman He planned for me to be. I have learned many lessons, yet God, in His miraculous way, is still revealing more of himself to me daily.

Some of what he has shown me is shared with you through my stories and poems in this book. I can only hope that you are able to glean a glimpse of God along the way and you too will be mended by the Master as you read these words.

Day 9
Of Stones and Snakes

Luke 11:11- What father among you, if his child asks for a fish will give him a stone, or if he ask for an egg will he give him a snake.."

CHILDREN ARE ALWAYS HUNGRY. WHAT do they do when they grow in a house where hunger is a crime, punishable by violence or with labels such as a belly robber? How could one rob a belly that is perpetually empty? The children in that house on Pioneer Trail were no different than any others, but there were rules about food. They learned early about the invisible locks on cupboards and on the refrigerator. Those places were forbidden.

But there were plots and schemes to garner food. The hero of the day award went to someone brave enough to sneak an orange up the stairs and share its juicy bounty with among the seven children who savored each drop, even eating the peel had its rewards.

But they were watched. Oh, the countless meals where he watched like a hawk circling a defenseless mouse as each dish was passed. One dare not put more than one small scoop on the plate for fear of the ever-ready backhandedness that plagued him. More often than not one of them was dubbed with the title of pig and knocked down for the count. He always demanded immediate recovery and the blessed one would crawl back up to the table to eat at the command to pull their fat belly back up. Bloodstains the mashed potatoes but because there is hunger, the child has the courage to eat.

Stones of harsh fear were a portion of the meal fare at the house. But for him, things were different. He accused his quaking wife of starving him. The children knew the truth...he was treated like royalty... or at least she tried. Oh, the parade of food that passed by between meals...toasted cheese sandwiches; thick chocolate milkshakes; BLT's and the bread slices slathered with Miracle Whip with a pickle or tomato. One can never forget the aroma of that forbidden food. Its aroma clung to the air and the children learned that a mouth waters more on an empty belly.

He could withhold the food but not stifle the imagination and they knew the smell would be the closest they would come to eating that night. You dare not look his way as he sat like a wolf hunched over its prey eating his morsels. One false move and he could snake over and dole out a serpent's bite.

The children of that house learned peculiar ways to satisfy their hunger as they grew older…. masking hunger with substitutes like alcohol, pills, attitudes, hang-ups, and always hurts. There was no safe place there so they eventually learned to find and secure for themselves safe havens that as they turned out were not so safe. Satan had cast a veil of apprehension over those children. A spirit of unworthiness as the most essential element of hunger refused to be met. Humanness was ripped from them slowly, painfully, yet surely.

These selfsame children are now adults, yet that hunger gnaws at them keeping them from feeling worthy enough; unable to receive without apprehension. Only one Father can heal their broken and scarred; torn and fill fitting garments. He can mend what another father tore. Just how He can make beauty from those ashes of the dust of hunger born disease is a mystery. I only know that He is able.

May these children, battered and torn, look to Him and be reborn.

To Eat His Bread and thus be filled
All the fear and hunger stilled
The house of stones and snakes is gone
In its place is the Father's song
A melody that soothes all pain
A broken vessel whole again

Day 10
The Gifts of Jesus

In an act of grace, Jesus tells about the gift of
the Holy Spirit. "I will not leave you orphans,
because I live, you will live too. My father will
send the Holy Spirit in my name and He will
teach you all things and He will remind you of all
I have told you. The gift of peace I give you and
it will be a peace that will not let your heart be
troubled. As you are in the Father, even as I am, I
gift you with the unity of being with me and our
Father as you abide in me, the true vine. I have
given you these gifts that your joy will be complete and full. When the Counselor comes the
Holy Spirit of truth you will be given the gift of
steadfastness, you will not stumble."
John 14, 15, 16

Day 11
Arms Wide Open

THIS MORNING I HELD MY ARMS WIDE open to a person I trusted to care. He looked straight and me and said one word, "Why?" Then he looked down and went about his morning routine. I felt an ax blow to my heart. Just another chipping away at what could have been a healing moment.

I imagine that's how Christ feels when he holds his arms wide open, totally vulnerable, totally honest in the invitation to love Him. Only a thousand questions of "why should I?" reverberate in his heart. As his body was scared before death, so His heart is scarred from the thousands of rejections. Small gestures of nonchalantly turning away from His arms that long to hold His beloved and He grieves when the object of His love turns aside to embrace the world instead of Him.

I run to Him in my pain and he heals another scar and says build your life around me, not your circumstances. I am reminded of the exiles in Babylon when Jeremiah wrote them a letter and challenged the exiled to focus their energies on how they could live their best life in the place where they found themselves. They could kick the dirt and feel sorry for themselves or they could get down to their knees and pray that they could live their best possible life in this strange land.

We can say "I'll do my best with what is here because God is with me." Eugene Peterson writes, "Change is hard. Developing of intimacy is always a risk...building relationships in hostile surroundings is difficult. But if that is what it means to be alive and human, I will do it."

God told the people through the prophet Jeremiah that he had a plan for his people, that he would "Put my law in their minds and write it on their hearts and I will be their God and they shall be my people." Jeremiah 31:33

Today, this day started with a rejection but will continue with love in my heart from God who is my strength and my portion. For "It is God who works in me to will and to act in order to fulfill His good purpose." Philippians 2:13. For my God has His arms wide open to embrace me and so I will live in the light of His love.

$\mathcal{D}ay$ 12
Jackfruit

MY NEW SON-IN-LAW PROUDLY CAR-ried into my kitchen, something that looked like nothing I had ever seen before. It was as big as a large ham but brown like an overripe banana. It had no smell but was covered in skin that could have belonged on an armadillo. It weighed about ten pounds. Wanting to put my best foot forward, rather than in my mouth, I asked, "what do we have here, Jeff?" He smiled a smile only a mother could love and proclaimed, "Jackfruit, since we are going on our honeymoon and we knew we weren't going to use it, we thought it would be good to bring it to you." Isn't that just like our children, always bringing us something they think we can enjoy? Sometimes it's dandelions then sometimes, well, it's jackfruit.

Well, off they went and there I was facing this thing just sitting there daring me to try it. Not knowing what else to do, I turned to my computer, thinking, let's find out about this. Pretty soon, I was watching YouTube videos with a hostess that looked like she was from India, explaining the wonderful nature of the jackfruit, how to clean it and how to eat it. A great deal of time and about a half a box of band-aids later, I was enjoying a delicately flavored fruit. It was wonderful and it got me thinking that maybe somehow that fruit is like some of the people we meet. They look different on the outside. Their shell may look uninviting but on the inside, they are people just like me. We may need to take a little time and effort but sometimes we can find something wonderful. Jesus calls us to love one another just as He loved us and He looks past the exterior and gazes at the heart, finding something wonderful. We are His masterpieces, each and every one. Let's challenge ourselves to the jackfruit in our lives and get to know the blessing of finding a treasure.

As for me, I can hardly wait for the next thing that child drags into my house. God love him!

Day 13
Healing Hope

Wherefore lift up the hands which hang down, and the feeble knees, and make straight paths for your feet, lest that which is lame be turned out of the way, but let it rather be healed.
Hebrews 12:12-13

CHILDREN WHO ARE BEATEN DOWN and trodden upon have hands that lie limp at their sides. Their heads and hearts are burdened by hopelessness, a sense that comfort will never come, that pain will continue forever. I was one of those children, behind the bars of my crib, only daring to peer out when I thought no one was looking. Only crying out when the anxiety and tension rose to a point of explosion. Then, it was only a whimper. I learned not to voice my pain to anybody. I could only whisper to myself again and again, "It's okay, it's okay."

But slowly, oh so slowly, I began to know that it was not okay for my arms to hang down, to slump. It was not okay for my heart to be limping and lifeless. The awakening was turtle-like because I ran like a rabbit from the pain. Once I learned to crawl, I could begin to exercise control over the delivery of the physical pain. I could begin to get away, first physically. But I could never escape emotionally. Still, there was no hope for the pain to end. It just had a new name. Again, and again I renamed it. I disowned it, delegated it, relegated. Hated it but loved it. It kept coming back because there was no hope for the baby in the crib, the child behind the bars, the prisoner.

The Greeks, they were pretty smart. Curious how they could come up with one word to describe a whole concept, an essence, a state of mind, Kairos.

An opportune, acceptable, favorable, legitimate moment in time to leave their old way of life behind and take up a new one. I knew for me, I had to first lift the hands which hung limp at my sides in my crib. Lifeless for years and fumbling for love between empty fingers that held only each other. I knew I was clinging to myself, my hands gripping each other and then hanging empty, forlorn, like my life, hopeless of ever being filled. Empty at my sides, flesh touching empty flesh.

This lifting of my hands in the crib to the hands of Jesus hurt. They had to travel through years of pain and mistrust and treason. Yet the time had come. Kairos. That moment I saw Christ appear in my room. Not my 41-year-old room, but the room of a baby. His hands reached into Priscella's crib. I saw hope like a great light. I understood Christ in me the hope of glory. Shadrach, Meshach and Abendego walked into the midst of the fire, knowing there was risk, but trusting God. Little arms reached to Jesus and trusted despite the risk.

Something wonderful happens. A part of the old man is being shed. A part of the new man is being woven into the mantle of my life. I know I can walk and my infirmities will be touched by the Master's hands. I trust him.

The pool of Bethsaida, the feeble knees, learning to walk in obedience. Learning to live and walk through the midst of the fire holding the hand of Jesus. I don't have to crawl anymore. My elbows are seared from the years of pulling myself around with my face to the ground. Enough! Kairos

I must not let go. I must not pull back. I must not stop trusting. The new man has a new purpose, a new Spirit, a new heart. Making straight paths will be a challenge.

It will hurt but I have not suffered unto the shedding of blood. Christ bore that agony. But to partake in His suffering means I must face my pain and pour it out to the Father, pray for new meaning, accept restoration and be willing for the resurrection from the dead works that engulfed me.

I am willing, Lord, to take self-corrective actions. Let my will, my self-will be of a creative and divine nature. Your nature, so that my paths are straight. You will help me walk the path. Your yoke is upon me. You will help me by Your Spirit, stay close to Your side. Hope springs eternally because of Your love.

My arms are raised in worship, receive my praise. My knees are bent in prayer, receive my supplication. My will is bent toward you, receive my life.

Day 14
Garments

Mender of the fabric
Minder of the soul
Labor of love
Gift from above
Work
By the scarred hands
Of sacred hands
That were held out all day long
Now hold up the worn
Weary and torn
Tatters and tears

Where the healing begins
The suffering ends

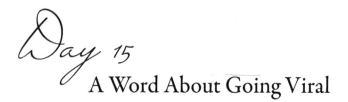

Day 15
A Word About Going Viral

*"I was at ease, but he has shattered me; He has
also taken me by the neck and shaken me to
pieces..." Job 16:12*

A ND WE WERE AT EASE, FOR THE MOST
part. We made our plans. We had our sched-
ules set, invites sent out, reservations made. We
had even begun to wonder how we were going
to 'do' Easter this year. Some had even ordered
that all important holiday ham. Stores were full of
Easter supplies.

Our church was getting ready too. After all,
besides from Christmas, it was normally peak
attendance time. Special programs were planned,
welcoming people instructed, Easter lilies lining
the pew. Funny how that works. It's almost
like a concession "a throw the old dog a bone."
Appearance at church on the holidays. Like they
gave God some attention almost in the same oblig-
atory way as you would pet a dog and say "good
boy" but never paying attention. Just a casual

encounter and a fiver in the plate and it's over and you can get to what really matters this time of year, March Madness and ham.

Just like Job, I was at my ease. Surgery scheduled, regular visits to my new granddaughter, juggling my calendar to get everything in and all of a sudden I was taken by the neck and shaken to pieces.

Seemingly, everything went viral everywhere. In turn, that virus was putting an end to my plans. It's like that verse in the Bible "He makes the plans of the people of no effect." Well, it's true. Being a senior citizen, I had special times I could go into Walmart or Giant Eagle donning a mask and gloves. I had to adapt to curbside pickup of meat orders at Duma Meats to minimize exposure to the virus. My freedom had been curtailed. My surgery got cancelled, my Medicare checkup cancelled. Changes, trying to adapt to these changes had been difficult.

I went to Giant Eagle on a Monday morning at the allotted 6 am time and there were people scattered everywhere. There was none of the normal rhythm of shopping. Some people went right to the toilet paper then cut over to meat then hurried over to milk. It was a mad house.

That Tuesday we went to Dumas for a curbside pickup that took all of the ten minutes to get. My reward for having spent four hours trying to get into the queue for a pickup time. I even got up at midnight to try to get an available space on the curbside schedule. But it got done.

A note of gratitude to the mail carriers, grocery workers, cashiers, cart boys, truck drivers, shelf stockers, radio and tv people, all those people holding things together. I am so grateful to them all. Did you ever stop to think just how many people it takes to put a jug of milk on the table, not counting the cow? The farmer who milks, the builder, the barn maintainer for the storage equipment, the man who drives the truck, the man who makes the jugs, the trucker who delivers empty jugs to the plant, whoever fills the jug, whoever carries it to the storage facility, the truckers who deliver the milk to the store, the clerks who stock, the cashier that rings it out and then I get to drink it. We should be more thankful. Many people were taking great risk to serve us during that time.

We have to adapt and be adept at it. This change had hit me most in my church life. The church is closed but God is open for business 24/7. There is a verse in Psalm 18:36. "You have enlarged my path under me, so my feet did not slip." On that larger path God had placed Pastor Scott Hindel, who was rapidly adapting and was giving us connectivity to each other so that we can corporately have church. I could hardly wait to see how we could all have communion together while we were apart. I just knew Scott would find a way.

On the day I wrote this, I prayed God's blessing upon the person who would read this. I asked that you find delight in our Lord as we had this time apart.

> *For who is God, except our Lord?*
> *And who is the Rock, except our God?*
> *It is God who arms me with strength*
> *And makes my way perfect.*
> *Psalm 18:31-32*

Day 16
Thirst Knows No Season

Psalm 63:2, "O God...my soul thirsts for you in a dry and thirsty land where there is no water."

I N 1922, THE COCA-COLA COMPANY launched an advertising campaign with the slogan, "Thirst Knows No Season" to run in the winter months to remind people that Coke was not just a summertime drink. Nine years later an American illustrator, Haddon Sunblom added an image of Santa Claus to the advertising campaign and thus the association of Coca-Cola with Christmas was born. Among collectors of memorabilia from this era, early ads and other promotional items featuring Santa and Coke are highly prized additions to their collections.

We are a thirsty people. We crave hydration products. Gatorade, Powerade, Propel and Body Armor are among the leaders in after workout drinks. Then there are hosts of pre-workout drinks designed to power up your exercise. There are hundreds of products meant to make hydration more appealing. Then of course there is Kool-Aid, Capri Sun, and an array of juice boxes and pouches to appeal to the youngsters. Then there's water, Dansai, Aqua Fina, Smart Water are leaders in the thirst-quenching business.

Of course there are the coffee conscious people who can't pass up Starbucks or Dunkin Donut to get their favorite concoction. Then there are the hard-core caffeine addicts that won't stop the mumbling to themselves in the morning until that caffeine meets their lips. Tea drinkers are a class of thirsty folk who can't make it through the heat without a chilled glass of sweet tea. Here too are a host of choices, Lipton, Celestial Seasonings, Twinings, and Harney and Sons, to name a few.

There are literally thousands of brands and flavors of alcoholic beverages from beer made in the mountains to beer made in microbreweries or alcohol aged for years in barrels.

And who could forget soda (pop in some parts of the country). Coke, Pepsi, Moutain Dew, Vernors and Crush, A&W Root Beer, 7-up and Dr. Pepper. There's hundreds of brands to choose from

Yet the people still thirst. Through all seasons and stages of this life. We start at the bottle, graduate to a sippie cup, then go to any of the above bottles cans or pouches attempting to satiate our physical thirst.

Yet there is a more innate longing that cannot be fulfilled by any liquid. It is a spiritual longing, a deep desire both to be known by God and to know God. "As a deer pants for water, so pants my soul for you O God. My soul thirsts for God, for the living God." (Psalm 42:1-2). Throughout thousands of years, man has had an inner urge, an inner suffering of sorts to find an answer for the thirst in his soul. Even when his mouth is no longer dry because he had a drink, his soul was still parched because satisfying physical thirst cannot reach into the dry places of the soul that long for streams in the desert. The Psalmist laments in Psalm 63:2, "O God...my soul thirsts for you in a dry and thirsty land where there is no water."

The prophet Isaiah writes in chapter 49, "...the Holy One of Israel has chosen you.. (He) will preserve you...(you) will neither hunger nor thirst... the Lord comforts His people and will have mercy on His afflicted." Years later the Holy One of Israel, Jesus, stood by one of His afflicted ones we often refer to as the woman at the well and offered her living water saying in John 4:13, "whoever drinks of the water that I shall give, him shall never thirst... (and) the water that I shall give him will become a fountain of water springing up into everlasting life."

What is unique about this water of life that springs into life eternal is that it satisfies our thirst for righteousness. Deep within our souls is a longing to be nurtured and loved beyond condition, beyond doubt in spite of our inherent nature to rebel against what is virtuous. It is this rebellious spirit that leads us into the dry places. The places that parch the soul.

Jesus said in His Sermon on the Mount, "Blessed are those who hunger and thirst for righteousness, for they shall be filled." Filled with what? Filled with the fresh, flowing, living streams of water from the depths of knowing Jesus. The ones that search for righteousness seek God daily; immerse their hearts into His Word and get filled. They are not satisfied today with yesterday's filling. They pour over the words of scripture until the newness of God's daily blessing are poured over them. As Jesus was breathing his last on the cross, he cried out, "I thirst." Though his body was suffering from dehydration, I can't help but think that His thirst was for the righteousness of His Father. For it is there that the thirst of the soul is satisfied. He knew where the pools of compassion originated from. It was sin, but the sin, our sin that prevented Him from finding refuge in those living waters. For He again cried out, "My God, My God why have you forsaken me?" His Father turned away from Him because Christ became sin on our behalf and the father cannot look upon sin and remain Holy.

There could be no relief for the Savior in order that there could be released from sin for His sheep.

Don't be content with the satisfaction of spiritual thirst from last week's sermon. Dig into the wealth of living water from the wellsprings of God's love daily, then you will be blessed daily with new strength in the roots of your faith. Remembering always, Christ thirsted so we can be overflowing with righteousness.

Pepsi had an ad campaign once that promised, "More Bounce to the Ounce." God's promise is greater still. "He who believes in me, out of his heart will flow rivers of living water." This living water can be renewed daily and it will satiate a thirst for all seasons of your life.

Day 17
A Culture of Senders

W E WANT TO BE HEARD. WE WANT TO be seen. In our quest to garner a voice in the spotlight we have embraced a culture of sending. We spend hours sometimes sharing our words and images into cyberspace through emails, blogs, podcasts, Facebook, Instagram and texts. Photos and words are displayed freely. We seek to be understood and seen and noticed yet it's paradoxical that we despair in our yearning for intimacy.

We readily anticipate the arrival of the mail or packages from USPS, Fed-X, UPS, and Amazon. We get excited about receiving yet we seldom get excited about the arrival of a person at our doorstep.

We need to get out of this rut of longing for intimacy and yet yearning for privacy and begin to become the hospitable people.

There was, in the early church, a developed culture of sending. One centered on the witness of the resurrection of Christ. Their vitality was wrapped around this idea of sharing, person to person, the good news of the gospel. The burning question was revealed in Romans 10:14-15, which, in essence, is a passage about the urgent need to send out witnesses into all the world.

Their heart's desire was not focused on receiving things of this world, but rather, as Paul says in Romans 10:1, "Brethren, my hearts desire and prayer to God for Israel is that they may be saved." This desire inspired by the Holy Spirit, compelled Paul, Peter, Timothy, Stephen and countless others to enter into the Spirit-centered culture of sending, It took them into the world to share this great gospel of faith in Christ.

Let us be a people full of faith and the Holy Spirit and enter joyfully into this culture of being sent as a witness sowing seeds of the gospel and of the grace of God.

Look up from your device and quit looking for that package to arrive. Look up for the fields are ripe for harvest.

> *Matthew 28:19- Go ye therefore,*
> *and teach all nations, baptizing them in*
> *the name of the Father, and of the Son,*
> *And of the Holy Ghost*

Day 18
The Greatest Teacher

1 John 2:27- But you have received the Holy Spirit and he lives within you,... the Spirit teaches you everything you need to know.

R EMEMBER WHEN YOU WERE IN SCHOOL and you had a favorite teacher, one you admired and listened to? One who compelled you to excel? You weren't distracted by note passing doodling or the snow falling outside. Your focus was on your teacher. You listened to his words and had a desire to display honor to him at exam time by showing him you respected his teaching by doing well on exams.

When we consider the role of the Holy Spirit in our lives he inhabits. Our every action, every word we say or think and each thing we do reflects how well we have been listening to the teaching of the Spirit. If the Holy Spirit isn't your favorite teacher, perhaps you need to consider if distractions of this life are grabbing too much of your attention. Is your focus on listening to the Holy Spirit or in listening to music, tv, or other voices?

Direct your focus on the things of God and pray the Father to allow your favorite teacher to be his Holy Spirit. He has something he wants to teach you, listen to it. You won't be disappointed when you focus on the Teacher.

Day 19
Peter the Rock

PREACHING FROM THE BOOK OF PETER, Pastor Scott invited us to ponder the thought of how close we came to never even having a book of Peter. Peter, that impetuous one who boldly proclaimed to Jesus in the upper room, "Lord, I am ready to go with you both to prison and to death," Luke 22:33.

That same Peter, when asked to watch and pray as the Lord prayed in the garden, was lulled to sleep as our Lord agonized alone. Matthew 26:37-46. That same Peter whose feet were bathed by the Master were the same feet that fled with fear from the garden. That same Peter whose eyes met the eyes of Jesus as the rooster crowed immediately following his third denial of Christ. (Luke 22:61) cringing inside and running out of the courtyard weeping bitterly (Matthew 26:75).

As he pounded his rough hand into the dirt screaming No! No! A thousand times No! He remembered his words to Jesus in the upper room and his pride and his sleepy eyes and flight from the soldiers his denials and raged into the night. But then, slowly, surely, the Spirit whispered back to him the words of Jesus to him. He was singled out, he heard Jesus saying, "Simon, Simon! Indeed Satan has asked for you, the he may sift you as wheat. But I have prayed for you, that your faith should not fail, and when you have returned to me, strengthen your brethren." Luke 22;31

Slowly Peter sifted through the master's words, but I have prayed for you...when you return to me... and little by little he was strengthened and eventually returned to the upper room.

That same Peter who responded to John's cry, "It is the Lord!" (John 21:7), plunged into the sea setting out to the shore where Jesus had prepared a charcoal fire (similar to the charcoal fire in the courtyard in Luke 22:54). That same Peter who in John 21:15-19 was asked, do you love me, three times. He answered three times, "Yes Lord, you know I love you." That Peter received a personal commissioning from the Lord: Feed My sheep, tend My sheep and you follow Me and follow, he did. In Acts Peter led the way in choosing the 12th disciple and paved the way for the proclamation of the gospel in Acts 2:14.

That same Peter, under the power of the Holy Spirit, authored two books of the Bible packed with dynamic teaching. His emphasis on having a sober mind and a unified body chosen by God, came from personal experience. His views on submission and humility come from his personal pain in his battle against pride. His sound advice to be sober, be vigilant because your adversary the devil walks about seeking who he may devour,(1 Peter 5:8) comes from his own experience of being sifted by Satan.

This same Peter strengthen and restored has much to teach you Christians. Study, dwell, immerse yourself in God's word so that after you have suffered a while (Jesus Christ) will perfect, establish, strengthen and settle you in these unsettling times. To God be the glory!

Matthew 16:18
And I say also unto thee, That thou art Peter,
And upon this rock I will build my church;
And the gates of hell shall not prevail against it.

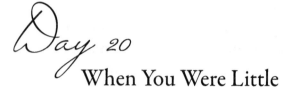

$\mathcal{D}ay$ 20
When You Were Little

When you were little in your own eyes...did not the
Lord anoint you King over Israel?"
1 Samuel 15:17-18

I NDEED, SAUL WAS HUMBLE IN HEART when he became King. He was willing to serve the Lord with his whole heart and not go after empty things. But slowly his heart turned inward rather than upward and after two years he told Samuel, " I felt compelled and offered a burnt offering." His performance of an act reserved for the Lord's anointed prophets prompted Samuel to tell Saul, "You have done foolishly...now your kingdom shall not continue (for) the Lord sought for himself a man after His own heart." 1 Samuel 13:12-14. In time, Saul began behaving rashly, making oaths and decisions which he hoped in his heart would restore his former standing with God. His waterloo moment came when he was commanded to utterly destroy the Amalekites yet he took their king named Agag alive and allowed his armies to plunder the spoils rather than destroy everything and everyone. Once again Samuel came to Saul and said, "when then did you not obey the voice of the Lord...and do evil in the sight of the Lord." Saul tried to justify his actions and was told by Samuel, "Behold, to obey is better than sacrifice... Because you have rejected the voice of the Lord, He also has rejected you from being king."

How often do we, when we are little in our own eyes, humbly approach the Lord and little by little start to drift away? Let this story be as a great warning to stay humble to seek after God's own heart in everything. Let us not grieve the Holy Spirit of God in anything we do or say. Let us pray without ceasing and find the will of God for today. Let us stay little in our own eyes.

Day 21
A Cloud of Dust

W HO DOESN'T LOVE THE FIRST WHIFF of spring? The warmer breeze tinged with winter's farewell scent beckons us to lift the windows, swing open the door and breathe deeply the promise of new beginnings. We pull up all possible rugs and take them outside to shake them. We turn mattresses and start washing the walls to chase out the cloud of dust winter has left behind.

Shaking the dust from our lives is almost a full-time endeavor. Over half of the dust in our homes comes from the great outdoors carried in on our shoes and clothes as minute particles from the air float around and attach themselves to our clothes and hair. It comes in the house through cracks and crevices in our walls, vents and windows. Of course our pets carry in a fair share of dust. We are a source of dust as we are continually shedding dead skin cells from our skin, our body's largest organ. Then there's dander. Those tiny scales of skin cells shed from our hair, skin and pets. These things make up a good portion of household dust as it floats about and settles everywhere.

Thousands of products have come and gone to be victorious in the on going battle to conquer the dust dilemma. Among the first modern inventions was the Dust Beater. Used to beat the dust out of a rug suspended on a clothesline. Its inventor, Melville R. Bissell went on to eventually develop the vacuum cleaner. The array of products promising a cure to the dust problem is broad and sweeping brooms, dust mops, dust mitts, dust slippers, microfiber dust cloths, and dust busters. Names like Electrolux, Kirby, Bissell, Eureka, Shark, Dirt Devil, Dyson, Hoover, Oreck and Roomba and more, all vie for selection in the battle against dust. Then there are a host of sprays like Pledge, Endust, and Behold that promise victory against dust.

Despite all the efforts to clear the dust out of our daily lives, it's really an ongoing battle in the physical part of our lives. But in our spiritual lives there is an on-going battle to shake the dust off the things that keep us from making progress as a Christian. When Jesus instructed His disciples, "Whoever will not receive you nor hear your words... depart...(and) shake off the dust from your feet." Matthew 10:11. In other words, leave them quickly as in a cloud of dust, forsake them as an expression of rejection. Leaving someone or something or even a place by shaking off the dust means you reject that which was in the past as a means of making a clean break, or seeking a new beginning.

It's a call to faithfulness in what you believe. There is a battle against the dust of our old man hovering over us ready to settle into a clean heart. We should always be in the business of dusting off the old and readying ourselves for the things of the Lord. Paul well speaks to the quest for obedience to new beginning. "One thing I do, forgetting those things which are behind and reaching forward to those things which are ahead, I press on. The upwards call of God in Christ Jesus." Philippians 3:3,14

Paul had, on many occasions, to shake the dust off and change directions. He was always seeking a new direction, a new beginning. In our lives we must continually shake off the dust and walk in the steps planned in advance by God. It is always a challenge to actively reject rejection and leave behind us a cloud of dust as we walk worthy and faithfully toward the goal of following in the footsteps of God.

In the words of the 1936 song titled "Pick Yourself Up," from the movie "Swing Time:"

> Nothings impossible I have found,
> for when my chin is on the ground,
> I pick myself up, dust myself off

Start all over again.
Don't lose your confidence if you slip
Be grateful for a pleasant trip
And pick yourself up; dust yourself off
Start all over again.

If you are dusty from someone or something, just arise and shake it off and get on with your calling. Walk away from the doubter and nay-sayers, the obstacles and the burdens and leave it all behind in a cloud of dust.

Day 22
M&M's

W HO DOESN'T DELIGHT IN A PACKAGE of M&M's? The bright colors and particularly flavorful chocolate combine to create a confection that is unmatched. Childhood memories are forged around the unique candy. I remember my first one well.

This iconic classic was developed and first produced September 9th, 1041 by candy magnets Forrest Mar of the Mars Company and Bruce Murrie of the Hershey's Company. Mars had the idea for a firm, colorful shell and of course Murrie had the chocolate. Together Mars and Murrie first manufactured the candy to be put in the mess kits of soldiers going to war. M&M's are still being used in this way as a confection for soldiers.

Advertisers had a field day when they developed the slogan, "Melts in your mouth and not in your hand." Some of the award winning advertisement features cartoon characters of M&M's and I still remember the ad where Santa meets the Yellow M&M and they both pass out just after saying, "He does exist!"

I imagine people have their own rituals when eating the candy. Some will eat them by the handful and just chew them up. Some will pour out the candy, separate them by color and selectively eat them color by color. I prefer to eat them one at a time letting the single M&M linger in my mouth until the candy shell is so thin that the rich chocolate just begins to melt. This way I discovered by lingering each color has its own unique flavor and there's the added benefit of having a package last all day.

While thinking about this, it occurs to me that lingering over the word of God can yield unique flavor with a burst of richness. Psalm 34:8 reminds us to "Taste and see that the Lord is good." We can't catch the full-bodied flavor of the Lord when our mind is set solely on finishing the passage. We need to tarry on the word, waiting in expectation of the richness that is in the shell of each word. Taking our time to dwell on its flavor, its meaning, making the passage last all day lost in study, meditation and journaling.

So next time you see a package of M&M's, there is an open invitation to tarry with the Lord, to be slow in parting from His word. When the Lord said in Acts 1:4, "Tarry in Jerusalem (and) wait for the promise of the Father." He meant for us to linger in expectation of the Holy Spirit. Try lingering over one M&M and you may begin to comprehend the mystery of waiting for the fullness of the flavor of God.

Day 23
Waterfalls

MILLIONS OF PEOPLE FROM ALL OVER the world travel to New York and Ontario, Canada to witness, firsthand, the mesmerizing majesty of Niagara Falls. There , in the presence of the roaring water, they are captivated by the sheer power inherent in the rushing of millions of cubic feet of water per minute continuously pouring over the rock formation. They are the source of continual cascading of power, an outpouring of ceaseless strength. Through the installation of hydroelectric power, plants, men have been able to harness nearly five million kilowatts of energy from Niagara Falls. Enough energy to furnish electric power to over four million homes daily.

As majestic and awesome as the outpouring power of waterfalls may appear, there is an even greater power that lies within the life of all who have put their faith in the Lord Jesus Christ. That is the power of the Holy Spirit. Jesus said in John 7:38, "He who believes in me, out of his heart will flow rivers of living water." He was referring to power of the Holy Spirit promised in the Old Testament through the prophet Joel who wrote, "and it shall come to pass that I will pour out my Spirit upon all flesh." This pouring is continuous in nature. It is an outpouring that flows unabated by things of the natural world.

The volume of waters flowing over waterfalls are affected by drought, natural disaster and ice and other forces in nature. Not so with the Holy Spirit. For the love and grace of God pours abundantly, powerfully, into our hearts through the presence of the Holy Spirit in our lives because of the finished work of Jesus Christ is a continuous flowing The resurrection of Christ marked the beginning of the fulfillment of the promised Spirit who would allow all who believe to experience the fullness of God.

All too often we let the fruit of the Spirit rot on the table set before us when our lives should exemplify the nine-fold fruit because of the living water rushing through our veins. Let us live empowered by the Spirit ever living to pour out of our abundance, Christ's love and grace into another soul.

"When the kindness and love of God
our Savior appeared...according to his mercy
He saved us through the washing and regeneration

and renewing of the Holy Spirit whom He poured
out on us abundantly
through Jesus Christ our Savior that being justified
by His grace we should become heirs
according to the hope of eternal life."
Titus 3:4-7

Day 24
An Itch You Can't Scratch

MEDICALLY SPEAKING, AN ITCH IS A symptom of an underlying disease such as psoriasis. It could indicate an underlying neurological disorder. Humanly speaking, there are times when we itch with a restless desire for something we can't identify. We're impatient wanting to do something. We crave relief. We look outside ourselves for a remedy for the itch we can't scratch. To satiate our longing we turn to substance abuse, shopping sprees, gambling, television, Facebook, all diversions that are temporary. What is unique to all of these are two things. They are external and in the end they do not provide the longer goal of getting the root of the itch. So we keep on scratching our way into deeper levels of disappointment and discomfort.

The people of ancient Israel were no different. They were looking to the things of the world to satisfy their itch. Their diversions led to them to seek foreign gods, substances, sexual escapades and other external pleasures. All to avoid looking for the internal source of satisfaction available in the heart of God.

The Lord sent prophets to lead them back to Him. Isaiah was a key voice for God for Israel. He said in Isaiah 29:30, "Woe to those who seek deep to hide...their works are in the dark." The people drew near to God with their lips but their heart was removed from God. They lamented to the prophet in Isaiah 30:10, "Do not prophesy to us right things. Speak to us smooth things."

Are we not the same? Those of us who itch? We want the smooth things, we want the smooth moves that will allow us to have a spiritually significant experience full of God but void of Jesus. Timothy well states in 2 Timothy 4:3-4, "For the time will come when they will not endure sound doctrine, but according to their own desires because they have itching ears, will heap up for themselves teachers, and will turn their ears away from the truth and be turned aside to fables."

What about that itch you can't scratch? Are the noises and distractions you're currently running to bringing satisfaction into into your soul? Have you yet discovered that you may be getting conned by your icons, your trusted solutions to your restless desire to scratch. There is a balm in the heart of God to satisfy the desires of your heart. The Lord waits patiently for your return. God will be gracious. The next time you have an itch, satisfy that longing by calling in the name of the Lord He's waiting for you now.

> "Therefore the Lord will wait
> That he may be gracious to you,
> That He may have mercy on you."
> Isaiah 30:18

Day 25
Soul Miner

IN 1867, ALFRED NOBEL RECEIVED A US patent on the invention of dynamite. His invention allowed great headway to be made in the mining industry. Miners no longer had to rely on crude inefficient tools like the pickaxe to access the wealth of coal, gold and other minerals. They now could put the power of dynamite to use to blast their way through hard rock. They could enter the heart of a mountain and harvest its treasures.

In the same way, the power of the Holy Spirit can enter the hard heart of man. In Acts 1:8 Jesus tell his disciples, "you shall receive power when the Holy Spirit has come upon you." The Greek word used here for power is dunamis. This is the root word Nobel used for dynamite. The significance of this power is that spiritually speaking, all men who have received the Holy Spirit, receive the ability to move the mountain of the rigid edges of a hard heart. They can, through the power of the Holy Spirit, become soul miners.

Back in the day when coal miners traversed deep into the mines, it was standard procedure to drill several holes then insert dynamite and light the fuse as they would run for cover against the power of the blast, they would yell out, "fire in the hole!" In a similar way, when the Holy Spirit enters into the heart, believers should shout out "fire in the soul!" Because a hard heart has been entered into by the Spirit of the living God. In the gospel of Matthew, John the Baptist testifies that, "He (Jesus) will baptize you with the Holy Spirit and fire."

Believers should be longing to be souls on fire for Jesus. He showed us the way. We can move in miraculous ways and with power. We only need to follow Him, light the fuse, and through the power of the Holy Spirit, be His witness so far as our life can reach. Go ahead, go in the power of the Spirit and be a soul miner. Through the Spirit that lives in your heart, move the mountains set before you and let your soul be on fire for the Lord.

Day 26
Considerations

"But Mary kept all these things and pondered them in her heart."
Luke 2;19

W E WOMEN KEEP MANY THINGS IN our hearts. From the ever-changing inventory of things to be done, to the wellbeing of our elderly neighbor. From the phone call we hesitate to make, to someone suffering illness or loss. Our personal heartaches and our profound joys. There is a constant rearranging of our lives to meet the unplanned, to respond to the urgent to whisper a prayer, or to react when the dryer alarm rings. We balance many responsibilities and we carry many things. We have many considerations. It is how we carry ourselves in the midst of the moment that changes the world around us.

There are times when our world seems so large and we want to shrink wrap the duties that call but we must consider our sister Mary who kept still in the light of all the activity in the small stable with the shepherds and the wise men and surely some towns people and she pondered everything. She must have thought, "This moment changes everything." She absorbed its wonder into her soul. As she was still in her spirit, so we must be.

In this season of our lives, let us consider Mary and as we carry on with our individual lives, ponder all that we carry and thank God that our load is made lighter by His love. May our souls absorb the wonder of the moments we spend with our loved ones and strangers alike as we prepare to make Him room in our hearts and we share the fruit of that preparation with others.

Day 27
Preparing Him Room

I WAS STANDING IN CHURCH, JOINING IN the well loved Christmas hymn, "Joy To the World" and sang, "Let every heart prepare him room." My mind drifted to the promise Jesus made in John 14:1, "I go to prepare a place for you." Then, instead of singing, my mind started wondering about the holy parallel here.

There is an urging in the song for us to be in preparation in our hearts to receive the newborn King. To prepare Him room, for He came to live in the hearts of men. Making room in our hearts is a serious matter. It really is something that we should do continuously as the world would entangle us in its snare of distractions. We have to make a conscious effort to dig out room in the heart. That room, as we mature in faith and grace, should be ever-expanding, ever-growing, always under construction with every sermon, every song, every event being additive to our dedication to Jesus.

In the meantime, Jesus is preparing room for us in heaven. He has said that we are not to be anxious for He gives us assurance that He will have a place for us.

While we prepare to be with Him for eternity, let us be faithful to make a whole-hearted effort to make ever more room in our hearts for Him.

Just as we are to prepare, so is He preparing a place for us in the heavenly realm. As creator, He is giving us assurance that He has a place for us and He will be waiting our arrival home.

Day 28
Light in the Darkness

S O, TODAY I'M IN A FUNKY MOOD. THERE really doesn't seem to be a reason for it. Doesn't it just seem if we could put our finger on the cause of our dark mood, like a miracle, things would brighten up? But no, perhaps I could contribute this mood to the same old grey sky spitting that intermittent rain. Bleak is the word I'm looking for. I thought reading my Bible would alter things. But no, still bleak.

Then I remembered a reading from yesterday's "Our Daily Bread" and I turned to a passage that got my attention. Its 2 Samuel 22:29, the NKJV reads, "For you are a lamp, O Lord. The Lord shall enlighten my darkness."

What a wealth of possibilities for my mood in this verse. The Lord is our lamp. He not only spreads a warm glow into our darkness, that light allows us to travel with Him step by step. The promise that the Lord shall enlighten my darkness handed me a gift. That word enlighten means to give spiritual insight and to instruct in wisdom. I mean, what more could we want?

Okay, so it's bleak. Let the warming glow from God's lamp battle the darkness. Allow the Lord to give you His wisdom and with his illumination in your spirit you can become a beacon of light to someone who may be having a bleak day.

Psalm 28:29 says, "He delivered me because He delighted in me," He delights to shed light in our darkness and deliver us from the pits we fall into. I feel so much better now knowing God is here right now for me. And he is right there for you too.

Day 29
A Taste for Stew

W E HAVE MOMENTS WHEN WE ARE weary, and we fall so easily into the temptation of the moment. Don't we have a bit of Esau in us when we yield to our hunger for immediate gratification? If you are looking to what is readily available, beware lest you satisfy the temporal for the sake of the eternal.

A taste even a morsel of the immediate often spoils the future fulfillment God has planned for you. God is not mocked for whatever a mean reaps begins with what he has sown. Whatever is sown to the flesh determines what is reaped in his faith... loss of an inheritance of righteousness is a grave neglect in the matter of grace and is detrimental to growth of the soul.

Then Jacob gave Esau bread and lentil stew,
and he ate and drank and rose and went his way.
Thus Esau despised his birthright.
Genesis 25:34

Day 30
In a Fog

I N LATE FALL IT IS NORMAL TO HAVE cold rainy days. These are the kinds of days that when you're driving you have to turn on the heat. Now when its in the low 40's outside and your vehicle heat is set at 70 degrees, sooner than later, the windshield fogs up. Sometimes it happens slowly, other times so fast you don't have time to adjust the defroster and airflow and all of the sudden you're driving blinded by the fog.

The other day was one of those days. I was driving on an interstate in a torrential downpour and my windshield fogged up to the point I could not make out what lane I was in. I put on my hazard light and rubbed a hole in the condensation. I could see lane markings but for a few minutes I was quite literally driving blind. I could see just enough to tell where the far-right lane was and cautiously, prayerfully, made my way over to the side of the road where I could safely stop. I grabbed a towel out of the back seat and wiped my windshield. The car had stopped where it would be easy to merge back into traffic again.

How I made it through the precarious situation is purely a credit to God. The whole time not one car honked at me. I don't recall there being any traffic around me at all during the whole time I was driving blinded and in a fog. Psalm 25 puts it this way, " Turn yourself to me and have mercy on me...bring me out of my distresses...for I put my trust in you." The Lord delivered me that day in a miraculous way.

When we trust God he constantly is present on our behalf. But every once in a while, He shows Himself to us in a powerful way. That day when I was helpless, he snatched me out of harm's way and while doing so He strengthened my faith in his steadfast love for me.

Later in the evening I was reviewing the events of the day and like a lightening bolt, it hit me, that I had requested prayer a week prior for safe and smooth transition for the re-location of my brother to a new nursing home some 35 miles away. God answered that prayer while I was driving in a fog.

Day 31
Wiped Out and Lifted Up

HAVE YOU HAD TIMES WHEN YOU FELT wiped out, utterly exhausted, unable to complete, let alone start, another task? Too wiped out to go another step, answer another call or carry another bag of groceries from your car to the house? It happens when we face change. Change alters us, transitions try us. It seems the urgency of the now and the exposure to the new somehow drain every ounce of reserve we have. Some attribute these times to stress. Times when our calendar is full and still there is an unexpected tug at the sleeve of our time.

Well-meaning friends and relatives tell us to just slow down. HA! Out of courtesy you say, "Okay you're right. I'll try thanks for caring." And no sooner are you leaving their drive than your mind is categorizing the priorities and once again you're off to the races stopping at the gas station for that over-due fill up and racing into the convenient store for milk.

Sometimes the most peaceful times we're afforded is that drive time when we breathe out a sigh of relief grateful for a few moments of silence. I reflected on the day. This morning I had woken up in a sour mood. You know how that goes. You're not mad, not sad, not bitter, just blah. I went through the motions of making my bed, letting the dogs out, taking my medicine, washing my face etc. Still not feeling with it. After I fed the dogs, I sat at my kitchen island with "Our Daily Bread" devotional. One verse caught my attention as I thought about the reading. So I started reading and rereading Psalm 3:3. "But you O Lord are a shield about me, my glory and the lifter of my head." I slowly got my nose off of the floor and stood upright because God is the lifter of my head. You could say God healed my spirit. He is the great attitude adjuster.

My job is to be faithful to remember He is my ever-present help. I remember tucking that verse away in my heart so I could remember that God is the lifter of my head. As I was driving, I was once again filled with a peace as I had been in the morning. It struck me just how quickly Gods truth can be overpowered by the pressures of the present. As I pulled to my driveway anxiety surrendered to peace and I was pleased and thankful to have been in the presence of the Lord.

$\mathcal{D}$ay 32
Whole in the World

"They tell me there's a place over yonder
Cool water running thru the burning sand
Until we learn how to love one another
We will never reach the Promised Land."
-The Eagles

A CCORDING TO WIKIPEDIA, HOLE IN the World is a song written by Glenn Frey and Don Henley in response to the attacks of September 11th, 2001. The song was released in 2003. This song rapidly reached number one status. It touched the hearts of millions, not only in America, but around the world.

Little wonder that we are drawn to the knowledge that there is a hole in our world. Not just because of one devastating event. It more than a global phenomenon, but also an individual experience. We all have a hole in our world. Each of us has an area or several areas where there is a lack, where something is missing, where the hollow nature of fear of loss or shame reaches into us and steals our sense of wholeness. We want to be complete; we too spend our lives looking for that part of the puzzle that somehow is missing and we can't break through the barrier of feeling incomplete long enough to find it.

On more than one occasion in the Bible we are given the knowledge that Jesus is willing to make us whole. His heart's desire is that we can come to a state of completeness and experience not just happiness, but joy. We can bring ourselves happiness, others can bring us happiness because happiness comes from manipulation of external circumstances: giving a gift, buying a house or a myriad of circumstances where your life is made a little less than ordinary by adding to it.

Have you ever noticed how much stuff you have, yet you're still lacking happiness? Whereas joy comes from within the heart. Joy comes from a sense of fullness or a feeling of completeness. It comes when an essential need of the heart is met. Joy builds joy...it's contagious. Joy multiplies itself. Jesus wants us to have a joy that comes from wholeness. He is that only part that can fill the God shaped hole in our hearts.

It was on a Sunday that Jesus came into the temple. He saw a man with a withered hand. The pain of the lack of physical wholeness touched the heart of Jesus and He asked the man, not do you want to be healed, but do you want to be made whole, a Greek word, holos, meaning complete, whole was used. Being made whole, the man jumped for joy. He was wholly complete.

With one touch from the Master you can be made whole. Your sins can be forgiven and with the help of the Holy Spirit each one of us can find that crazy missing part we have been searching for. Keith Green writes in "Your Love Broke Through," "All My life I've been looking for that crazy missing part and with one touch you just rolled away the stone that held my heart."

Jesus is waiting to touch you, to complete you, all you have to do is reach out your hand. There you will find cool water for your soul.

Prayer: Lord forgive my sins, I reach out to you, I want to be wholly yours.

Day 33
The Nature of the Perfect

T ALKING TO THE DOCTOR'S OFFICE, I confirmed to her the date and time of an appointment and she responded, "Perfect!" As I finished the call, I thought of her response and just how common it is today for people to use the word perfect in a rather odd way. They say perfect when taking your order at the restaurant, when choosing nail polish color or in response to a variety of situations. The use of the word perfect is quite common in common vernacular.

Even in the Wizard of Oz, Dorothy, after oiling the tin man under the tree, said to him when he started to move his arm. There, now you are perfect. I sometimes think his response should have been a bit more like, "Perfect? What do you mean perfect? Just bang on my chest if you think I'm perfect." He was the travelers on the yellow brick road who was missing a heart. He responded to Dorothy something like, "I have no heart. How can I be perfect without a heart?" She thought him perfect because he had been oiled and could move, but he knew he was incomplete, lacking a component vital to a vibrant life.

The primary definition in the dictionary is that perfect is something without fault or defect-flawless, or complete. The implied meaning being that something that is perfect is satisfying all requirements. The Greeks used the word perfect in reference to persons and often states of mind. The common Greek word teteoise means perfect, whose primary meaning reflects today's understanding of the English word. Variations of this word appear in the Bible. One of the most interesting use is in the word tetelesti used as Jesus died on the cross. The English rendering of this word is it is finished, indicating that a state of completeness had been reached, i.e. the work was perfect, the sacrifice complete to pay a penalty for all sin for all men for all time thus paying in full completeness our debt for our sins. That's true perfection.

When you hear someone use the word perfect, stop to consider the original intent and for a moment reflect on the impact of the finished flawless perfection on the cross. Ask yourself if you just might be lacking a component vital to having a vibrant more complete life. Remember if your mind is stayed on Jesus you will have the opportunity to find perfect peace and the nature of perfect.

Reflecting on the overly common use of the word perfect by our culture. I thought of the meaning of the word. Websters defines perfect as being entirely without fault, flawless. There is an implied meaning that something that is perfect is satisfying all requirements. I thought of what it would take to be flawless. Certainly nothing we can make or create can be flawless. That belongs to the realm of God that's reflected in the finished work of Jesus on the cross.

Day 34
Lost and Found

Luke 15:21-
For this my son was dead, and is alive again;
he was lost, and is found.
And they began to be merry.

I WAS PERPLEXED, UNABLE TO THINK what to do, where to look. I felt I was at the end of all my mental resources and all I could think of was that wedding ring. I had taken it off and as I was getting ready to put it in its usual spot, the phone rang, and I got distracted. The call was from a friend who was going through a hurtful time of separation from her mate. As I look back on it, I recall sitting down at the kitchen counter totally engrossed in our long conversation. My thoughts and prayers during our hour-long heart to heart were intense and I was feeling her pain in my heart by the time we said goodbye. The last thing on my mind was that ring.

The next day, as I went about my daily routine, getting ready for the day and reached for my ring.

It wasn't there, that dish that held it was empty. My stomach churned within me as I searched my mind for possibilities. Then I remembered the engrossing call last night. Had I misplaced it in my haste to answer the phone? What had I done with it? Distressed, I began to hunt for the lost treasure both physically and mentally. After a few frantic hours, I began to feel the dread of losing that ring. I was reduced to search, wait, and pray mode. I was afraid of having to face a tremendous loss.

Several days passed when an idea popped into my mind. I had a faint memory of what I did. I felt lightheaded hope and headed into the downstairs bathroom. I reached up to the top of the cabinet and sure enough there it was. Now, after those hours and days of agony searching for the lost ring, I found it. It was sitting on an old soap dish I placed up there. I vaguely remembered putting it there out of the way in a safe place where it wouldn't accidentally get knocked down the drain or off the sink. I had just forgotten. Rejoicing, I called my friend to share the good news. I had rest and peace in my heart. What was lost was found.

Telling this story, I am reminded of the heart of God for what is lost. How He must agonize over the lost. The Bible tells us of the return of the prodigal son. Recall how very much joy the father had when he saw his son. He had to burn with the fire of a holy hope that his lost son would be found. He never gave up. He remained faithful to seeking what was lost and as his son appeared in the distance, he ran rejoicing because what was lost was found. He called for a celebration. The Bible attests that there is rejoicing in the presence of angels over the salvation of one sinner.

If you're in anguish because you are lost, if you have come to your wits end, worn from brokenness of sin, remember, Jesus came to seek and to save the lost and He cries out, "Come to me and I will give you rest." God is ever ready to celebrate you home.

Day 35
Delete: Its Pain and It's Power

Who hasn't accidentally deleted something? You're faced with the awful truth that there is just no way to get back that message or email. Sometimes it's a personal disaster. What was saved no longer exists. You must go through the effort to re-create it and even then, somehow your original thought is changed. The original intention is changed, altered, revised. For man, restoring something back to its original form once it's deleted is out of the question.

Webster defines "delete" in this way, "to eliminate especially by blotting out, cutting out or erasing, i.e, Delete a passage in a manuscript, delete a computer file or an email.

For God, restoring man to his original form is possible thru the work of Jesus Christ on the cross. Jesus deleted our sins. He removed them far from us as far as the east is from the west. Isaiah writes in chapter 43:25, "I am he that blots out thy transgressions…and I will not remember thy sins."

Our faith in Jesus makes this possible. Believe on the Lord and you shall be saved. Your sins will be blotted out. They will be deleted by the grace of God. You can be made righteous before the throne as faultless as Adam before sin entered the world. You can be the original creation, God purposed before the foundation of the world.

Acts 3:19 states, "Repent, and be converted that your sins may be blotted out." Now that is cause for rejoicing. You can, as my pastor says, be justified, made just as if I never sinned. You can be redeemed and brought back. We can have a new vision of the word delete. It's ultimate meaning, spiritually speaking, is we can have a renewed vision for our lives i.e. Living for the one who died for me because of His great love.

The next time you're prompted to delete something or find out you mistakenly deleted something, remember Jesus Christ purposely deleted your sins and pause just for a moment to be thankful to the One who died to blot out your sins and restore you as if you never sinned.

Psalm 103:12-As far as the east is from the west, so far hath he removed our transgressions from us.

Day 36
Gadgets That Could Change the Way We Live

Revelation 21:5
And he that sat upon the throne said,
Behold, I make all things new.

IT SEEMS TO BE IN OUR NATURE TO anticipate the new. We get excited looking forward to a new year, new clothes, or a new job, new start, etc. Who doesn't experience that rush of excitement when our Amazon package arrives, or we get a new message or a new Facebook or Instagram notification? We crave the new and hunger for the temporary joy of having the newest gadget out there. We tire easily of updates because no sooner do we get them these days, but they have become outdated, superseded by a new, better, faster model. Given the choice, we select products touting labels like "New and Improved!"

We are like children waiting for Christmas morning, ripping off wrappers containing our wishes caught up in the excitement of finding what you hoped for but still grabbing for more. We're like hungry wolves whose kill satiates the growing hunger for more forces the hunt for the new prey. It seems the quest never ends.

We long for new beginnings, for a brand-new day to dawn. We even embrace self-help gurus searching for the "New You!" Always, darkness descends, the new becomes old and often forgotten, and that urge awakens and the longing returns. In our flesh, we are weak. It is bent toward the lust of the eyes and pride. We need a lasting, new beginning. One that has no shelf life and is resilient, one that is new every morning. We long for a newness that is continually refreshing to our thirsty soul; a breath of fresh air that comes, not from vial and a diffuser, but one that captivates our hearts and satisfies our longing for something that is infinitely unique.

For thousands of years, the Old Testament Jews were guided by the Ten Commandments. They tried to make them new by adding to them new levels of prohibitions and new ways of living the same. New Traditions were tacked onto the old ones. There were no new other new beginnings, just promises and prophecies that something new was coming, something that would make all things new. This promise of a new heart and a new spirit was the kind of improvement anyone would desire.

Then, it wasn't until Jesus came, that the Jews and all men alike might anticipate new beginnings. In John 13:34, Jesus added a new commandment. He said, "A new commandment I give you, that you love one another as I have loved you." Jesus is the Master of the new. He is telling us to love as He loves. When we can grasp this powerful concept, we can start fresh in all our relationships. Unlike self-help guides with their videos and DVD's, it was a self-help concept with God as a guide sending an example, a replication of Himself to teach this new way of thinking. He walked as we walked, was tempted as we are and was acquainted with our griefs. His love, God's love, leads to peace and peace to contentment. When you're not so eager for acquisition of the new, the content of our lives yield delight in the Lord. The Bible promises, if we delight in the Lord, he will give us the desires of our heart. What are you desiring? Do you desire a new and improved life coming from having of something new, or a new enhanced life coming from being renewed by the Savior? Do you want to glory in the abundance of things that grow old or do you want to glory in an abundant life being continually made new? Ezekiel 11:19 and 36:26 state that the Lord says, "I will put a new spirit within you...a new heart will I give you." His mercies are new every morning.

Don't settle for a new gizmo, gadget or gim-mick. Remember, if you're in Christ, you are a new creature. The old Is gone and all things are new and they are becoming new each day and moment as you put on the new man as you grow in grace and in the knowledge of the One who restores us. He makes all things new.

Day 37
The Rock Won't Move

I WENT UP TO MY CHURCH TO BRING some supplies for the food pantry on one winter, Saturday morning. Having a lot of things to carry in meant multiple trips from the car into the church. My first trip in I saw a rock on the ground by the door. My first thought was to roll the rock over to the door with my foot so I could use it to prop open the door. So, I kicked the rock to start to move it toward the door. Alas, it was frozen to the ground. "The rock that won't move," I uttered. As I was bringing things in, the pastor came along and offered help. I called out, "I tried to prop the door but the rock won't move!" Just then, in an instant, I was struck by how true that is of God. He is the rock that won't move. He is our stronghold, our cornerstone and our place of comfort and safety. 2 Samuel 22:47 shouts, "The Lord lives! Blessed be my rock! Let God be exalted, the God of my salvation." He gave me joy as I thought on how solid of a foundation He is in my life. The blessings of God come in many ways. Just a few simple words about

a frozen stone became a warm precious reminder
of God's constant presence in my life.

Isaiah 28:16
Therefore, thus saith the Lord God,
Behold, I lay in Zion
for a foundation a stone,
a tried stone, a precious corner stone,
a sure foundation:
he that believeth shall not make haste.

Day 38
Narrow Margins

I WAS DRIVING ALONG ON A LOCAL STATE highway at about 58 mph, with a car following a bit too close for comfort. I noticed a large truck on the left backing out of the oxygen supply depot ahead and the thought crossed my mind that he may just ignore on-coming traffic and proceed to back out of the driveway. After all, his cargo was cylinders full of oxygen and was precarious and if I would run into him there would be tragic circumstances. About 30 feet away now, he stopped just for a second and proceeded to back out. I think he may have been a few cups of coffee short of awake because he clearly was not thinking. Fortunately, as I first envisioned the potential for an accident I started to slow down as did the driver behind me slowed. By the time he backed into my lane, I slowed down enough to avoid impact. I thank God for His grace and giving me the wisdom to envision exactly what would have happened.

Grace hovers over us in our best, worse and all of our ordinary circumstances. This side of heaven we are often blind to his protective presence in the midst of our lives. At that moment, I was aware of His presence and was grateful.

Later in the day I was reading Job and I noticed how in Job 20:19, he cries out in desperation, "...I have escaped by the skin of my teeth." I was reminded of the incident earlier in the day how I had escaped by a narrow and fragile margin. God has cast a safety net around my life as he had done with Job setting boundaries that Satan could not cross.

Someday I'll enter into eternity with Jesus as my safety net, my covering for my sin. Not only in death but in life, Jesus is our shield, our defense against the wiles of the devil as he aims his darts of distraction and destruction against us.

God certainly had me in the palm of his hand that morning protecting my mind from some frivolous thought, Jesus gives us clarity of thought, renewing our mind continually as we travel in life along the thin, fragile line. That narrow margin that separates the very air we breathe from eternity.

Day 39
Nothing Breaks Like a Heart

I WAS ABOUT TO GET INTO THE SHOWER after a hard workout and heard the lyric to a song say the words, "nothing breaks like a heart." I knew I had to learn more about this piece of music. Wow, I thought how very true those words were. When I got home, I listened to the song, a collaboration between Mark Ronson and Miley Cyrus who first performed their hit song, "Nothing breaks like a heart" on December 7,2018.

But they weren't the first to record a song with that title. Back in the late 1970's and early 1980's an English-American rock band, The Pretenders, recorded a song with the same title.

Reflecting on these things I thought that as long as man has existed there has been this overwhelming need to express his feelings in words about the state of his heart. This need is reflected in not only music but in poetry, books and various other forms of art. Not matter how words are woven together there is still a void in the completeness of the expression of broken heartedness.

There are stirrings in the soul that remain word-less, expressions so deep that only God can reach. There is pain so deep that it knows no voice, only groaning utterance of the soul and it is a place that only God can go. Could it be that the reason for chaos is that we have not allowed God to enter into us, into our deep places, our secret spaces where our scars are nursed. Loss haunts us and its pain hunts us down until we give in to God.

The Bible tell us that He heals the bro-ken-hearted and binds up their wounds (Psalms 147:3) and when you make known to Him your secret spaces together with Him you can make them sacred places because there, He will mend your heart. You can be freed from the pain of the shattered glass of harsh circumstances because He ever lives to reach out to bind up your wounds with the freeing power of His love. Jesus knows nothing breaks like heart.

Day 40
A Fall To Remember

" ..In my distress I cried out to the Lord ..and my cry came before Him, He delivered me because He delighted in me ." Psalm 18:6,19

IS THERE ANY DAY FINER THAN A COOL crisp day in autumn when leaves sparkle with the firework colors and their rustling raises a refreshing breath of fresh air? The laughter of children playing in a pile of freshly raked leaves, the unique smell of burning leaves, the brief glimmer of gold dust inherent in the yellow aspens, and the colors that seem to glow an invitation to take in the beauty of fall.

There are the unique tasks of autumn-the clearing of flower beds, the planting of springtime hopefulness with the burial of tulips and daffodils, the raking of seemingly endless piles of leaves and the task that usually falls last on the to do list- the cleaning of the gutters.

My brother Harvey was one such gutter cleaner and apparently there he was, up on the roof diligently cleaning, when he lost his balance and fell off the roof onto the air conditioner and from there, onto the ground. It happened fast and fierce as most accidents do. Stunned, his flesh freshly filled with the fear that gripped him the instant he knew he was going to fall, he lay there in a heap, like a freshly raked pile of leaves. As he lay there, he felt signs of life and knew he couldn't just lie there in the back of the house alone. Summoning the depth of his resolve he crawled first to the back corner of the house. So far to go to get to the front yard where his wife could see him. Slowly, with agony he embarked what seemed to be the longest mile. He didn't know the extent of his injuries and was in far too much pain to call out for help, he endured until his wife came into view.

Thank God she saw and understood that he was in eminent danger. She rushed him to the hospital where it was revealed he had broken nine ribs- two in multiple places, plus broken his scapula. Twelve breaks in all. The doctors told his wife that after the age of 65 life expectancy drops dramatically for each break after a total of three. This was a fall to be remembered in a very dramatic way.

His situation was even more compromised as he had been diagnosed with a serious case of COPD-which made every breath a supreme effort.

Churches were contacted with urgent requests for prayer. God was with him and he made it through the first night.

The next day was Thanksgiving Day. I canceled my plans and went to the hospital. The image of a pale faced man with oxygen being supplied to him was stark and stays in my memory. Surely this wasn't Harvey my beloved brother-but it was. I sat in silence with Nancy as the doctor went into specific detail of Harvey's chances of survival.

Hundreds of petitions went up to our Lord for mercy and deliverance. Meanwhile Harvey continued in his fight for his life breath by breath. At first being helped by use of four liters of oxygen and slowly his need for supplemental oxygen decreased, until he was down to needing only two liters of oxygen then praise God and Harvey's valiant efforts he was weaned from the oxygen and could breathe well on room air. In a few more days he would go home and continue the battle.

All the while, we continued in prayer for his healing and comfort and the Lord delivered him from the pit. It was truly a miracle that he survived such a blow to his 70 year old body and I praise God for His steadfast love for one of His beloved children, in whom He delighted.

We never know, do we? When without a warning we will slip and fall, when circumstances will lead to a full blown threat to our lives, but

God knows and He is ever ready to stand beside us and encourage and love us into acceptance of His perfect will. We need to mirror Gods love to those around us because we never know when we will encounter a fall to remember. When my faith fades the Lord reminds me of the mile marker my brother passed and the Lord's faithfulness to him and my faith is refreshed and renewed Because of that fall and God's grace I am assured of His love for even me . Sacred moments such as these hold a secret placed in my soul anchored to the hope of an ever-loving Savior who, by his abundant grace delivered His faithful servant Harvey, that Fall to remember.

Day 41
Erasing the Slate

SLATE IS AN INTERESTING STUDY. Basically, it's a dense, grained, metamorphic rock produced by compression together of various sediments such as clay, shale, minerals or even volcanic ash, in a unique perpendicular plane. Metamorphic simply refers to a rock that arises through transformation of existing rocks. Metamorphosis is commonly used as a word to describe the transformation of a chrysalis into a butterfly. What is unique about slate is that it splits along parallel planes allowing it to be harvested in long sturdy sheets. Its highly non-porous surface makes it an excellent material for pool tables because slate is the only surface material that can be leveled to $1/10,000^{th}$ of an inch, thus creating the smoothest surface known to man for the accuracy of the rolling ball. It was first used in 1826 in pool tables. Close to that time, in Vermont in 1848, the first slate roof was installed. Slate was even used in the late 1880's for use in schools.

Regardless whether the slate is the superior Italian variety or whether it comes from Wales or Vermont, it is still considered a coveted material no matter how it's used. But what about the slate that your life is written on? How do we summon up the courage to erase the slate and as they say, start over with a clean slate? How we choose to erase the slate has a good deal to do with what is on it and how deeply it's etched there by times of going back again and again rehearsing the lines of our bitterness, brokenness, losses, lies, hurt, pain of rejection and neglect, emptiness, anger, anxiety, all those enemies of the soul that damage our spirit and stifle our potential.

That slate of bondage can be wiped clean in one and only one way. Oh you can try rubbing it off but vestiges of the original sin against you, whether self-inflicted or not, remain until you allow the forgiveness of the Father to wash you clean.

This forgiveness is both a miracle and a mystery. A miracle because while Christ suffered and died for our sins, he was resurrected to new life, a new life that you never in your wildest dreams imagined to be possible. Because of Christ's forgiveness, you can experience a metamorphic phenomenon, the old becoming new, the mind being renewed daily as you partake of His Word. Your food for thought erasing those enemies of your soul. A mystery because when we understand the forgiveness we have received from God the father, we become able to offer a gift of forgiveness to the one who caused harm to scar your life. You can reach a pinnacle of faith that allows you to pray, "Father, I look at the cross now and I know I have asked for and received forgiveness for my sins against you which are many; who am I, a sinner saved by grace, to not forgive that person who sinned against me?

David prayed in Psalm 51, "Against you only you have I sinned and done what is evil in Your sight. Father, create in me a clean heart and renew an upright spirit within me." God gave David a clean slate, a chance to start over and he is willing to give you a clean slate. Won't you come?

Day 42
Running on Empty

I KNEW I WAS RUNNING ON BORROWED time, but though I was nervous about it when my gas gauge was near E, I still panicked when the gas light came on. To make matters worse, I wasn't quite sure when that light came on. I was mentally calculating miles to the nearest station while trying to remember what the hastily read owner's manual said about the number of miles I could go before the car ran out of gas. Come on, who really reads that manual unless they have to?

Of course, every light was red, which meant more idling time. Then, to make matters worse, the words "Low Fuel" popped up on the screen. I could picture myself pulling to the side of the road and walking to the station paying 25 dollars to use a red plastic container then in walking back to the car which would probably have a ticket on it. Why, oh why, did I let this happen?

As I turned into the station, I breathed a sigh of relief. I felt like that station was my oasis in the desert. As it ended up, that car took 10.80 gallons to fill. Then I resorted to look at the manual and found out its fuel capacity was 11 gallons. I had a very close call, all because I put off something as simple as filling up my gas tank.

I'm reminded how often we let the simple tasks undone today and before we know it, we're in crisis mode, full of anxious thoughts about what could possibly go wrong. This brings to mind the words of Jesus about anxiety: therefore, do not be anxious about tomorrow for tomorrow will be anxious for itself. Sufficient for the day is its own trouble. Matthew 6:26.

What is so significant here is that the day I saw I was in need of gas, I did not take action. I did not attend to the task at hand. If I had taken care of the trouble of today, I would not have been thrown into a state of alarm in the future. How often do we end up with a stack of unopened mail, unmade phone calls, unopened emails, and undone chores because we didn't heed the warning light of God's word to take care of the sufficient tasks of today. We leave our unopened Bibles unread, devotionals until a tomorrow that will itself be full of its own worries. We procrastinate and then wonder why we don't have the energy to take on anything new.

Someone once said, "Life is so daily" and I thought how simple that was to understand. I think what he was meaning has a lot to do with that scripture verse and how important it is to take care of the things of the present thus avoiding the anxiety of the undone. There is much to be said about the old adage, "never put off till tomorrow the things you can do today." Tomorrow will bring its own set of circumstances. What we need to do today is stop ignoring the advice of the Lord about today's troubles. Paul tells us in Philippians 2:4, "Let each of you look not only to his own interests, but also to the interests of others." When we do, not only are we prepared to order our own lives, but we make room to be mindful of the Lord's business and avoid the calamity that running on empty brings.

Day 43
Starting Over

R EGRETS, WHO DOESN'T HAVE THEM? Remorse, who hasn't felt it? How often do we long for another chance to start over? But all too often we find that piece of baggage we have carried around is still stuck to our hands. We try to pry it off but it just won't come loose so we make the same sorry mistakes, walk that same weary road, clinging to that same particular burden. That burden carries within the only bag of tricks we know to escape life's tough circumstances. We try to change but as long as we cling to the tried yet not so true methods, we will never find lasting relief from the regrets, remorse, hurts and brokenness that consume who we really are and reveal all we were meant to be. What we need is to be restored, we're in desperate need of a make-over because with life there is no such thing as a do over.

Maybe that's a part of why the hit television show, "Fixer-Upper" held many of us captive. Interior designer Joanna Gaines helped us see the possibilities of the improbable. She and her husband Chip demonstrated show after show that they could alter, improve, create and breathe new life into a structure and make a house become a home. Gaines continues to help us see possibilities through her Magnolia enterprise. She shows us that restoration is possible.

Starting over is possible, but like the show "Fixer Upper", sometimes walls have to be torn down, garbage has to be taken out and hauled away, and baggage has to be released because you'll need two hands to do the work. You'll also need qualities like patience and endurance as you commit to labor to show yourself approved. God is in the restoration business too and has been from eternity past. Think of yourself as a fixer-upper project that only God can restore. You come to him just as you are and he has promised he will make all things beautiful in its time. Could it be that your time is now? Isaiah 55:6 entreats us to seek the Lord while He may be found, to call upon Him while He is near. God is just as near today. You too can be restored and renewed because God's not finished with you yet. So roll up your sleeves and get to work!

Day 44
The Whole Nine Yards

THE ORIGIN OF THIS PHRASE, MEANING giving everything, going all the way, is unknown. It's a colloquial English phrase which may derive from a saying analogous to the whole kit and kaboodle according to Wikipedia. Some of us may be familiar with the crime comedy film entitled "The Whole Nine Yards" released in 2000 and starring Bruce Willis and Matthew Perry.

Another similar term is one used particularly in the early mid to 1900's and occasionally you'll hear it today when someone says, "they always dressed to the nines," which means perfection. In the film "The Great Gatsby", the characters were always dressed to perfection.

When I think of perfection, I think of Jesus. When I think of someone going the whole nine yards, going all the way, giving everything, being all in, I think of Jesus at the cross. He was wholly devoted to saving us from our sins. 1 John 2:2 says, "He is the complete perfect substitute (propitiation) for our sins.

Hebrews 10:9 tells us that Christ offered Himself up as a single sacrifice for all time for all sins. I often imagine what agony he carried knowing in advance the intensity of pain He knew would suffer. Like a woman carrying her second child, she knows from the beginning the travail she will experience at birth. But she sets her mind on the goal of the joy set before her, not on the pain or the discomfort to come. For the joy set before her, she endures the pain. Then when she holds her child the pain is a thing of the past. When Jesus holds us, he too is filled with the abundance of joy.

Jesus knew what pain He would endure, yet he bowed his heart and head to the will of the Father so that for the glory set before Him, He suffered and died so each of us could have new birth. This goal was His ultimate joy. This is why He went the whole nine yards.

John 3:16
For God so loved the world, he gave his only son
That whoever believes in him will not perish
But will have everlasting life.

Day 45
Good For the Soul

EVERY ONCE IN A WHILE, YOU'LL HEAR the phrase, "work is good for the soul." According to the author Frank Sonnenbergon, hard work build character and promotes courage, dignity and develops humility.

Now we know according to Ephesians 2:10, that we are his workmanship created in Christ Jesus for good works which God prepared beforehand that we should walk in them. Doing the works God's prepared for us builds our Christian character.

We see over and over again the qualities of courage, dignity, and humility in our Lord as He walked in the path prepared by God for Him. Because of His works, we witness His grace. We are encouraged, perhaps commanded to follow Him. To walk as He walked always being mindful of the works laid out beforehand. His mindfulness of His works kept Him focused on the Father.

The reward of our works is not a paycheck but a payout from God unto our soul. A spiritual deposit of dignity, humility and character. We sense in our souls an accumulative balance of grace that magnifies the voice of the Spirit within us that echoes, "be strong and of good courage." That voice is music to our souls and feeds our hunger for more.

What works has God prepared for you today that you should walk in them? Am I walking in the Spirit so I may have the eyes to see and the ears to hear the nature of works awaiting me today? How hungry is my soul for the blessings of grace inherent in the works designed for me?

Let us be hungry for those works for they are good for the soul that yields the desirable fruit of the Spirit, that fruit which is a delight to heart and spirit that satisfies our hunger and thirst after righteousness.

The challenge is to walk in the path prepared for us, walk thusly and you will find rest for your souls.

Day 46
I Decay...

I WENT INTO THE MCDONALD'S TO GET A coffee with my brother Harvey and the cash register girl was looking quizzingly at the cash register saying what I thought was "I decay, I decay." My mind started searching out why she would be saying such a thing. After all, aren't we all, while we're living, in some form or another of decay? Dental decay, moral decay etc. Then I thought of a poem I wrote about the descent of King Saul into deeper and deeper sin. He started out so good (don't we all?) The first king grew into a proud and jealous king overcome with bitterness and eventually to the point of consulting mediums. Anyway, Saul saved some special spoil to sacrifice when he was told by Samuel to utterly destroy the enemy. He was on the proverbial slippery slope toward deterioration. Imagine the arrogance of Saul sacrificing spoil to the Lord! Samuel caught him in the act and reprimanded Saul with a simply profound statement that should ring constantly within us: "to obey is better than sacrifice." It is more obedient to give the 20 dollars to the widow or sacrifice that 20 to the offering plate? Didn't Jesus say to take care of the widow orphan? When do we start with partial disobedience and end with complete decay. When does our silence about our faith become Saul's falling on his sword? The poem line went "a darkness overcomes them as they're slowly led astray. When partial disobedience becomes complete decay."

Back to Mcdonald's, I said to the girl who was saying "I decay", "what do you mean by that?" She responded, "You know, IDK." She was confused about a menu button and was speaking the text lingo IDK meaning I don't know. But interestingly, I though about decay and the poem and Saul and myself. How much decay do I have in my life when I listen to self and not the Spirit? How about you? Do you know? Are you aware of your own IDK quotient in your spiritual life? Lord help us all as we live for Him and not the spoil.

Day 47
Making Holes Whole

THE FRONT PAGE HEADLINE IN OUR local rural paper was "Pothole Patrol." The bane of our NE Ohio roads has drivers on alert near the end of winter playing dodgeball with the multitude of potholes that crop up as the roads expand and contract due to changing weather conditions. The only way to fix these is to get out the orange barrels and resurface the road and we all know that creates its own hazardous and annoying conditions. Those potholes seem to plague us.

Some etymologists seem to think they are labeled potholes due to stories of potters in Britain digging into the roads to harvest the clay laid during Roman occupation days leaving holes in the road. Drivers would then curse the potters for leaving pot shaped holes in the roads.

There is no way to patch ones of these holes without leaving a lump or bump in a once smooth surface.

Potholes are akin to the sins left lurking in the souls of Adam and Eve. There was no way to completely restore their once pure lives. They are like the holes sin rips in our lives. They can never be restored as if it never happened without the redemption offered by Jesus' work on the cross.

If the road ahead of you is hazardous and crated with the many potholes and pitfalls of daily life, turn to the Creator for restoration. He has promised that, "if anyone is in Christ he is a new creation. Old things have passed away, all things have become new." Only He can make a soul marred by the holes of sin, whole. And He has not orange barrels for us to dodge.

Day 48
An Open Heart Policy

W E LIVE IN THE AGE OF THE INSTANT. Innovations like Instagram and Instant Messenger have made our lives seem faster than a speeding bullet. What was once relegated to be a quality of Superman is now seemingly unspoken regulation in regard to an unwritten code of cell phone etiquette.

The age of the instantaneous and automation has brought the Instapot, the remote starter, the Roomba, Alexa, self-check-outs, echo dot, firesticks, to name a few. It seems like everything is smarter these days. Innovation galore! Hardly a day goes by without a new quest for something to make lives go easier and faster. But are we any smarter?

Still, in the heart of man, there is nothing new under the sun. No new way to get tired, angry, hurt, sad, impatient and fearful of trials. No new way to avoid temptations. The problems, challenges, and joys of living haven't changed anymore, nor have they changed any less. There is nothing new under the sun. Sin is still lurking at our door and like our ready response to the new, we seem to have an open-door policy. Let's call a spade a spade.

Our hearts, desperately wicked, are tempted to grasp any new idea that comes along and like the brass rings at the fair we grappled to pick of the newest apple of our eye only to find we tire of its taste and want something more satisfying. We are ever tired and thirsty for more.

We want the abundant life but are distracted by too much busyness to contemplate the source of a life that is full, and we want it instantly. They say change doesn't happen overnight. There's a dilemma. We want it now but have to wait. Real change is a process of transformation. The source of an abundant life is God. We are to steadfastly seek Him. To rejoice in hope, be patient in tribulation and instant in prayer (Romans 12:12)

Instant in prayer. There's our concept! One that should be our guide, our roadmap of life app. Bringing every thought into captivity of Christ requires instantaneous thinking. We look outside ourselves for the instant solution when it was there all along. We change our open-door policy to an open-heart policy and allow God to change us instantly moment by moment.

Day 49
God's Gift of Knowledge

A S WE STRIVE TO SUPPLEMENT OUR faith with knowledge today, it is crucial to be aware that we all recognize, all the things we know in our heart come from divine revelation. Words travel through our minds at a rapid clip but it takes our Teacher the Holy Spirit to turn those words and yes, even circumstances, and transform them into knowledge of God's will for our lives today. This way, wisdom is not wasted through the passing of random words, but it is invested in growing up our hearts into Christ's image.

Our goal is spiritual perception of the truth of God's words. Something more than facts accumulated in the mind, knowledge is discovery of facets of God's character which prepare our hearts in season and out of season to glorify God in our hearts.

Today, seek knowledge in order to bolster your faith and broaden your understanding of the greatness of God. Give all diligence to this most excellent of endeavors, that you might know Him and the power of His love for each member of His body. Walk in unity with His Spirit today.

Day 50
Living a Virtuous Life

VIRTUE, THIS FIVE LETTER WORD, though a small word, carries a wealth of morality and a challenge to Christians to partake in the divine nature of God. In order for the divine nature to manifest , the believer is to make every effort to supplement their faith with seven qualities the number seven signifies completeness. The first of these is virtue. Virtue enables us to conform to a standard of righteousness, a moral excellence or goodness. Let us strive as a body in unison to excel in virtue today so that you are continually sowing what is right and good into the lives of all you encounter today. Let our goodness glorify God today.

Day 51
Self-Control is Spirit Driven

TODAY'S SPIRITUAL SUPPLEMENT IS self-control. We are instructed in 2 Peter 1:3 to add to our knowledge, self-control. This quality of character is to be added to our faith so we might increase our understanding of the Word of God. An uncontrolled self is liable to be impulsive and thus wander quickly away from the truth of God's precepts and lured into the following of doctrine that sounds good but in the end is a dried up stream. Without this quality, we are weak in our resistance to sinful desires. It is crucial to understand that self-control is one of the nine-fold fruit of the Spirit. Self-control for the Spirit-filled believers is produced in you as you follow the urging of God. We must carry about in our hearts this aspect of our divine nature as it is cultivated through the divine power given unto us through the working out of our faith in the death, burial and glorious resurrection of Jesus Christ. Today, listen to the voice of the Spirit as He guides you through the treacherous path of the desires of the flesh. Include the Holy Spirit in each step you walk today and the result will truly be victory in Jesus over the sin that so easily entangles us. Walk with the goodness of virtue in the wisdom of God in submission to the Spirit's prompting and that you will earn restraint over your impulses, emotions, and desires and you will discover self-will subdued as you receive the blessings of self-control.

Day 52
Hunger in the Land

HUNGER, THAT CALLING OUT OF THE cells of the body for nourishment, strikes at times when we are seemingly unprepared for it. But there is also a heart hunger where only words spoken by the Lord will fill the empty crevices where the life has been sucked out of you by circumstances beyond your control.

What do you do when you seek the Lord and it seems like He is hiding from you. He hears but doesn't answer. You call His name and only hear the echoes of His name bounce around inside of you. There will come a day, bitter as bile rising to your lips, when you will cry out and only hear the silence roar. Amos warned the Israelites in chapter 8:11-12.

"Behold the days are coming, says the Lord God, that I will bring famine on the land, not a famine for bread, nor a thirst for water, but of hearing the words of the Lord ...they shall run to and fro, seeking the word of the Lord, but shall not find it.".

He states that in that bitter day, the Lord will make the pain of separation so sharp it will be like mourning for an only son.

We must remember that the Lord wants our devotion, our undivided love for Him to be our portion. So call upon Him while He is listening.

When we take the broader path to satisfy our desires, we may find that we get hungry from our journey and our broader path to satisfaction may lead us into the narrow crevice where our heart cries out for the Lord but we have been gone too long living a life of ease that not even a word from the Father can be found. Though we may be surrounded by all sorts of sumptuous morsels, we find there is hunger in the land.

> *Take heed what you hear...whoever has,*
> *to him more will be given; but whoever*
> *does not have,*
> *even what he has will be taken away.*
> *Mark 4:25*

Day 53
Contentment

Now Godliness with contentment is great gain. 1 Timothy 6:6

A S WE CONSIDER BEING FRUITFUL IN growing in the faith, we take pause to consider contentment. That quality of being satisfied. It reflects the results of contemplating the sufficiency of being at ease internally with the qualities added to our lives by diligence in allowing virtue, knowledge, self-control, perseverance, and godliness to invade the crevices of our hearts

Contentment would not be complete with allowing brotherly kindness to permeate our lives. We consider the gift of adoption into God's family and must consider all believers to also have been adopted into this royal family. Wouldn't it be a forgone conclusion that we would act with kindness then toward all believers who are brothers and sisters? Yet we find through the weakness in our flesh, kindness eludes us on occasion, and we fall into fault-finding and pettiness.

It is for this reason that Peter urges us to be diligent about adding brotherly kindness to this recipe for a stronger faith. Our faith is stronger when we stand firm together and proceed in one accord. This mutual kindness promotes unity of the body, glorifies Christ, and moves us as one toward unshakable faith.

Let us have brotherly affection, caring for the wholeness and wellbeing of all segments of mankind we encounter so we can be "Great at the great commandment" and continue to follow Christ by loving God and loving others and ultimately serving the world. Now that kind of contentment is of great gain indeed.

Day 54
Begotten Through the Gospel

"BE IMITATORS OF GOD AS DEAR CHIL-
dren and walk in love." As children often
mimic their parent's characteristics and behavior,
we should strive, as children, begotten as sons
through the Gospel, to carefully study and mimic
the characteristics and behaviors of our Father.

Our spiritual supplement today is godliness.
As spiritual sons and daughters, we strive to imitate Christ, meditate in his virtues and goodness
until you believe by faith that Christ is in fact our
brother. He told Mary at the tomb, "Go and tell
my brethren to go to Galilee and there they will
see me." Adoption into God's family shows us
the greatness of God's love for us and our gratitude for this high gift of grace of adoption should
spur us on to imitate the behavior and character
of our Father thru sharing the gift of godliness.
Godliness should shine as a beacon of light and
hope to the world around us. So today, let the
Holy Spirit shine on through you as you walk in
godliness.

But godliness is profitable for all things.
1 Timothy 4:8

Day 55
The Race isn't always to the Swift

T HERE IS AN OLD CHINESE PROVERB that advise us to "Behold! The turtle only makes progress when he sticks his neck out." So what does that have to do with making every effort to supplement our faith with perseverance? Plenty! Turtles on the move are characterized by steady, earnest and consistent effort in their attempt to make progress, they have to practice what Eugene Peterson calls long obedience in the same direction. They are diligent in their efforts to move and they take risk because they have to place their most vulnerable part outside of their protective shell.

We are all familiar with the fable to the tortoise and the hare. The hare was swift but foolish. Whereas the tortoise was focused and steady practicing continued effort to achieve victory by persistently moving toward the finish line. The hare got distracted by the cares and temptation to linger in a field of carrots while the tortoise steadfastly progressed. You see, the tortoise took his spiritual supplement of persistence seriously. He was driven by self-control and didn't get sidetracked. He fixed his eyes on the goal and became a winner in the race much to the proud foolish rabbit's dismay.

As we travel our road today, let us be focused on the goal and hold steadfastly to our faith always looking to Jesus, so as we run our race we practice continued effort to share in the divine nature and allow that nature to penetrate our lives and "run with endurance the race that is set before us" Hebrews 12:1. Let us be bold in the living out of the gospel sticking out our necks , progressing and walking worthy of our Lord. Persevering in trials, overcoming obstacles by faith, consistent in well-doing, and in knowledge obtained by divine revelation, follow in the footsteps of our Savior.

> *Do not neglect the gift that is given to you*
> *Give yourself entirely to them*
> *That your progress may be evident to all*
> *1 Timothy 4:14-15*

Day 56
Sowing to the Flesh

S o, once again I find myself angry about a situation beyond my control. Though my logic tells me if it is out of my control, why live in anger mode? Since when do I listen to logic? Well into anger mode, I faithfully read my Bible and oh the irony of it all. So I read, "whatever a man sows that he shall also reap. For he who sows to the flesh will of the flesh reap corruption..." Galatians 6:7. It hit me like a ton of bricks... ouch! I was reaping anger in my flesh because I was reaping what my mind was sowing! While I've been busy sowing anger, I have missed the depth of living a life of peace. I have been stuck in the shallow water missing the baptism of blessings God had in store. Then I read this note in my Bible: Convictions always guide us back to Truth so we can keep in step with the Spirit. So it is with a lighter heart I turn from the sin of anger and repent and I am so thankful for the Truth shining upon me this moment.

Day 57
When Sleep Steals Prayer

T HE CHILL OF FALLING NIGHTTIME crept into the bones of the three disciples. Asked, "Stay here and watch with me, for my soul is exceedingly sorrowful." Watch for what they wondered as they saw him from afar fall onto His face. They pulled their thin garments tighter against the ensuing darkness and closed their eyes in prayer. Heavy hearts make heavier eyelids. And they drifted into sleep. A mindless escape from the cold reality of all that had transpired and the frigid anticipation of what would be.

They were startled awake with one word, 'What?" Even they could not believe their failure. When Jesus said, "could you not watch with me one hour?" Again they were told to watch, instructed to pray, lest they enter into temptation. They were humbled when Jesus said, "The Spirit is willing yet the flesh is weak." As Jesus went again alone to pray, the three, with renewed resolve, huddled closer, encouraging each other, wondering what temptation could arise. Together their prayers filled the air as Jesus was a distance away. Yet again, as the evening fog, chilling the air and stealthily slipping into their midst their prayers became slight whispers as their eyes grew heavy. They were lulled into a deep sleep. Seeing them sleeping a second time, Jesus left them and prayed fervently to the Father and He came back to His three beloved disciples sleeping and resting.

"Arise" he said with urgency. Half awake, hearing the word betrayer, their hearts fell with shame within them. They had already begun the descent, the fall into temptation. Peter, as if to redeem himself, drew the sword and blindly struck out. As if in a nightmare they swayed in slow motion as chains bound Jesus' hands and feet. That they had just been bathed in love, now fled in fear. Their hearts beat wildly within them knowing now full well why they should have watched and prayed. That what was foretold had begun. And sleep had been a thief of more than their prayers.

Day 58
No Deceit

No deceit was found in His mouth
Nor in His heart
For that is where deceit is born
Nor guile-that cunning mind
That device of mischief
That guile was absent
Behold Nathanial an Israelite
In whom there is no guile
Is there even one Nathaniel
Among us
Whose lips do not drip with guile
With devises so thorough
That reveal a heart of deceit?
Even on the cross His heart
Was pure, forgiveness laden
Grieving over the lost
As he breathed his last.
Oh! To be so pure
To be transformed in heart
And mind that we wear His mind
Without deceit.

It is an unreachable goal
A brass ring on a carousel
As the horses race

To the same tune
Can we sing a new song
As we chase after Jesus
As we reach for the prize
Of the upward call
Being void of deceit?
Can we suffer to gain
Victory over cunning
To claim the crown of glory
Nathaniel personified
And hear as he did
About the coming of Angels?

$\mathcal{D}$ay 59
Scattered

Nothing is more
Mysterious nor
Notorious as the
Dandelion.
It's bright
Yellow is often
The first sign of spring
Enchanted children
Pluck its blooms
Running to their mothers
With a fistful bouquet
Enraged gardeners
Attack it with Round-up
Only to find it's
Unyielding tap root
Undanted
Returns
And blooms
Quickly turn to
Fluffy seedlings
Swiftly scattered

By a child's breath
Or a gust of wind
The seeds disperse

With random abandon
And soon
Again bloom in
Lawns and fields
Believers should note
The tenacity of the dandelion
Mimic the dispersal
In all directions
They too should
Have tap roots
Entering deep into
The soil of their soul
Impossible to uproot
Persistent to bloom
Patiently scattering
Seeds
Impervious to poison
Focused on the dispersing
Seeds of the gospel.

Day 60
The Infant and the Infinite

On the outskirts of nowhere
The angel came
To tell of an infant
Jesus would be his name
He spoke words of wonder
He spoke of a Son
"rejoice you will carry
The infinite One.
Blessed are you
And full of God's grace
This child will save
The whole human race."
"Let it be unto me
Just as I have heard
For I believe that you're speaking
God's holy Word."
With a perfect contentment
She prepared Him a place
In her heart as she pondered
The depth of God's grace.
Peace overcame her

As the angel withdrew from her sight
And the Son of God was conceived
On that Holy night.

In the middle of nowhere
In a place without fame
Our Savior's form was beginning
Immanuel his name.

Day 61
A Simple Church

A heavenly vision
Is shaped as we pray, and
The Holy Spirit leads the way
Under the guide of the
Word and prayer
We find ourselves in
The Father's care
If we listen, we will hear
"Follow me" whispered in our ear
Become what you have seen in Me
Loving God for eternity
In this love see other's hearts
And serve them as the Spirit imparts
Continue in love and serve until
You plainly see the Father's will
Follow Jesus in all you say and do
And bring others to come along with you.
A vision seen becomes reality
When we love the Lord relentlessly.

Day 62
Reflecting His Image

God drew a breath
And the Holy air it
Brought forth
Spread
With an artful purpose.
It's aroma wafted
Floated and flooded into
The form of man created from
Minute particles of dust passing thru
The fingers of the Father
Air bequeathed
Breath
Breath bequeathed a living soul
Endowed with the mind of God
With
Creativity without limits
Imagination crystalline in its purity
Emotional satisfaction
Eternal security.
Earnest ability to serve
Void of the plagues of doubt or fear

Perfect submission
Flawless union
An endless harmony of truth
And grace.

The man walked worthy of his calling
In the path that was blameless and
Ministered to the creator with a heart
Full of humble thanksgiving
And endless joy for
The purity of a perfect heart
Reflecting His image
He found the yoke to the Father easy
And the burden of perfection light.

Day 63
Gratitude

Oh! For the grace to
Offer up gratitude when
The way is darkened
By the tears of the soul

Blessings come and
We rejoice in their pure light
The unknown blocks
The light
It clouds the vision
Of the radiance of faith

Uncertainty is a plague
Of doubt and fear
It's veil blocks
Our weakened hands
From grasping the essence
Of God's steadfast love

Oh! To give back to the Father
The gratitude of our soul

To offer from a purity of heart
A sacrifice of thanksgiving
When that sacrifice costs
Him dearly

Oh! To have a heart of praise
When there are days
Blessing cannot be
Remembered

Awake my soul from your slumber
Recall the days of joy
Came to visit my heart
Rewind the joy of your salvation
To the presentation of grand gifts of
Gratitude for the grace by which Christ
Declared you free

Give thanks for the handiwork of the Master.
You are His
No matter how dark the way
It will be brightened when
With a humble heart and whispering voice you say
"I'm grateful Lord this is my choice"

Though the path seems hard
Walk worthy of the call
To offer up your best
To sacrifice it all

Day 64
Even though-Yet I will Praise

Though the fig tree fail to blossom
Even so Springtime will return

Though there be no fruit on the vine
Even so your cup will overflow

Though the fields yield no food
Even so you have the bread of life

Though the flock be cut off from the fold
Even then the Shepherd will search for all
who are lost

Though there be no herd in the stable
Even so your meat is to do the will of God

Though all is stripped away
Though He slay me with sorrow

Even then I will rejoice in the Lord and
I will take joy in the God of salvation

Though I am weak and confounded
Even then the Lord is my strength

Though I am weak and confused
Even then the Lord is my strength

Though my feet tremble and slip
Even then He imparts unto me deer's feet

Though he takes me on the high places
Even then I tread firmly on the pinnacles of the fear
of the unknown

For I trust in Him
For I will rejoice

I will take joy in the God of my salvation
And I will rest in Him

Day 65
Silence Breaks

For when I kept silent, my bones wasted away
Through my groaning all day long
Psalm 32:3

T HE HEART IS NOT MADE TO HOLD silence in, the body is racked with the inner pangs refusal to speak can bring. We are meant to share our secrets with the Almighty who searches our hearts. When we don't, silence eats us up alive.

Silence breaks like shards of a broken mirror. It multiplies reflections of unspoken pain. There are no words to utter when joy is executed by a haughty look or the acid of accusation. Silence cannot find it's voice. It is lost in the forsaken heart. That hidden part troubled by a perfect storm wake of self condemnation, rebounds in surf of suffering churning undertow sucking the very breath of the soul that is forsaken by rejection.

Only Holy ears hear the inner groaning and speaks the balm of comfort.

Silence turns away, silence lies, it ties the tongue, it anchors the soul in the dark pit. Silence is the hurricane that washes up yesterday's debris in its wake. The breaking just a little more. An already ravished heart

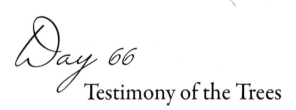

Day 66
Testimony of the Trees

One tree in Eden
In its beauty arose
From the Creator's hand
Full in repose

It's root grew deep
Nurtured by God
It stood mighty but gentle
Embraced by the sod

It stood in its wonder
Both in power and might
To discern the difference
Of the wrong and the right
It's well tended branches

Bore a fruit that looked sweet
Eve reached up and took it
And the fruit she did eat
The pure became tainted

Sin entered her heart
She offered to Adam
And that was the start

A tree meant to hold
A knowledge divine
Was used by Satan
To tempt
All of mankind

Now sin had entered
The heart of all man when
The prophets foretold
The intent of His plan

He brought forth to earth
The birth of His son
Light into darkness
The unfolding begun

His steps they were measured
As planned from above
The broken were healed
By God's greatest Love

All prophecy filled
Jesus came to the tree
Prepared in advance
To set us free

The tree was not lovely
It was barren and bare
Except for the Savior
Nailed to it there

Thought it yielded no fruit
The one hung in disgrace
Bore fruit for all of
Forgiveness and grace

The drops of His blood that
Watered the ground
They fell for us all
So we could be found

The cruel tree stretched His limits
"It is finished" He cried
His soul paid sin's debt
As the son of man died

The tree stood in darkness
It's duty was done
Soaked with the stain
Of the sacrificed son

The tree on Golgotha
Stood still and alone
The work done upon it
For sin did atone

God's plan was accomplished when
The stone rolled away and
He rose in glory
On the third day

The work of these trees
Was over and done
Man's salvation from sin
Now freed by the Son

Jesus is waiting for you to come
To the cross to be free
From sin's burden we carry
Both you and me

A tree of life's nourished
In heaven above
By living waters
And by God's love

Food for all nations
Fruit from its blooms
Every soul welcomed
There's plenty of room

Sins curse is finished
The Lamb is enthroned
He sits with the father
Upon Heaven's throne

A tree in the garden
One near the grave
The tree of life's waiting
For the sinner now saved

Drink from it's rivers
Holy and pure
Rest now in assurance
That salvation is sure.

Day 67
He Holds My Hand

In the darkness of night
He reaches out
He holds my hand
When the answer's not in sight
I know He has a plan

In anguish from my pain
When each heartbeat
Brings sorrows tears
He shares my fears
He understands as
He gently takes my hand

When trials overtake me
And press on every side
Confused and drowned
In questions
I'm at the limits of my faith
To humbly abide

Fears anticipation
Trembles every breath
My heart could be one beat away
From impending death

With a thread of trust
I tremble as I stand
As I reach for a bit of hope
My gentle Savior takes my hand
The Father takes my hand
Cling to him fragile spirit
He waits for you to come
He leads you every single step
As you travel home

And when I cannot bow the knee
And I'm totally undone
He makes his Presence
Known to me and
Gently reaches out his hand
And lifts me up to heaven's gate
Into the promised land

Day 68
Return

Come let us return to the Lord...for he will heal us
Hosea 6:1-6

We're off the path
We go astray
We follow after
Another's way
We wander off
The road to life
We wonder why
We have strife
There is direction
To be found
But we must ask
And turn around.
God chose a hill
For you to climb
It's path is narrow
It's route is divine
Try though we might
To shorten our route

God's hand is ever
In wonderous pursuit
He heals when we're weary
From pursuit of the Son
Keep climbing the path
The battle is won

Day 69
Surgery

God reached down from heaven
The day my life was spared
No complications simple
It was worse than it was feared

The doctor knew the instant
That my vitals changed
That the planned procedure would
Never go the same

All the learning garnered
Experience through the years
Caused the team of experts
Let wisdom conquer fears

A quiet calm descended
As the team assessed the storm
They labored as one together
Overcoming fear from chaos born

The doctor's hands inside me
Clamping off the flow
Of life's blood trickling from me
While I was breathing slow

His gentle hand held me
While in the grip of death
Light and darkness hovered
While I took a breath

All saints were praying
Lifting prayers above
A soul returned from heaven's gate
Because of his great love

A voice rings through the silence
I'm not finished with her yet
I've breathed in her the breath of life
She's rising from the brink of death

There's great peace in knowing
This battle has been won
The preservation of a soul
By the doctor and the Son

The terror of a moment
Is over in its time
He guides the hands of the doctor
And now he's guiding mine

I take great joy in knowing
He loves me even still
I'm alive, my soul is well
Because it was His will.

Day 70
The Glow of Grace

Have you ever touched the Son
Felt the warmth of his embrace
Heard the silence of the wind
Felt the glow of amazing grace

Have you ever truly heard him
when he calls you to come near
Can you leave it all behind you
Or listen to the voice of fear

Can you see that he is gentle
Feel the darkness turn to light
By the Spirit of the living Lord
Power of Gods glorious might

Have you ever really touched Him
He reaches out his healed hand
Grasp Him now the spirit calls
Glorious gospel to every man

Oh the glow of glory
Light from the living one
Shine on us we pray to you
Let us rise to the risen One

Oh the glow of grace
Holy Spirit in your heart
Embrace all of God in one accord
Father, Holy Spirit, Lord

And Jesus said, Who touched me?
Luke 8:44

Day 71
Misplaced Desire

*...David remained in Jerusalem...and walking on a
roof, he saw a woman bathing...then David took her
and lay with her.*
2 Samuel 11:1-4

Sometimes the wanting
Is better than the having.
Sometimes that desire
That fire
That burns till you blister
from its pain and its yearning
is best left smoldering.

Sometimes the having
Bears its own burden
The let down of
Unfulfilled longing of sin
That scars the soul
From the pain of
Too much too soon.

Anticipation morphs
Into disappointment
When reality fails to
Meet expectation
And the wanting into waiting
For having what was dreamed of.

Sometimes the wanting
Alone should suffice.
Sometimes the having
Reveals a vice, a peculiar ice
That refuses to thaw anew
A frozen purity.

Day 72
Torn

Mourn the missing children
Their stifled cries
Their stilled smiles
Premature death screams from
Unsuckled mouths
Their mothers pride
Has driven the unmerciful sword
Into innocent flesh

Racheal rise up
Refuse to be comforted
Rebel against the modern-day Herod
Wail against the wall
Of indifference to life

A cruel euthanasia
Accepting
A death void of dignity
Is deplorable

Day 73
Come As You Are

Come unto Jesus
If you are weary and worn
Come as you are
Have peace from the storm
Come down from your fortress
He'll stay at your home
He welcomes all sinners
You're never alone

Come now and follow
Lay your life down
Cast off your burden
Trade your net for a crown

The fields ripe for harvest
The workers are few
He's seeking to find
Someone like you.

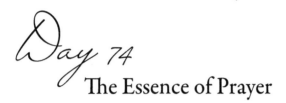

Day 74
The Essence of Prayer

Descend with the mind
Into the heart
In silence still
The roaring of the present
And enter the Presence
Of the Father
Let the secret places of the soul
Become sacred spaces
And bow the knee
To the Lord of all
Let the Spirit guide
You into the knowledge of
The will of God
Surrender all the burdens
Of the flesh
And feast upon the
Harvest found in
The presence
Of the Father

Day 75
Crucified

Listen....

TO THE MOB MARCHING TO THE GARDEN.
Hear the swing of the sword slice into the flesh of the servant's ear. To Christ taking quivering flesh and restoring it to its rightful place. To the wisdom of the God who would have Jesus' last miracle be restoration of hearing.

Listen...

To the chains, the crunch of the gravel, the swing of a fist as it meets sacred flesh. Hear the fire crackle as the smoke of denial clouds Peter's vision. The murmuring of the shadows lurking amidst the mob. They dare not step into torchlight. Their deed too is cloaked in darkness. Feel them pushing in for a closer look at the suffering of the Savior. Soldiers cackling, pushing, jabbing. Their taunts fill the night air. Hear the hatred of the false priests as they rip their robes crying "Blasphemy!

Away with him!" To Herod's jesting. To Pilate's testing the waters, for a political resolution. He wants no blood on his hands.

Listen...

As a would-be executioner grunts. The cruel whip sways again and again. While the flesh of the Lamb is torn. Bone against bone. Hear Pilate say to the crowd, "Who shall I free?" And the crooked generation cries, "Barabas!" Hear his garbled laughter. The muffled cries of the women are drowned out by the frenzied echoing, "Crucify him!"

Listen...

To the labored breath of the One sent to die. Hear His tired feet shuffle beneath the cross as He stumbles through the sand. Listen to His broken body falling, turning the sand red. Groaning beneath a weight He was born to bear. The whip whistles as He rises. Hear his body scale the mount. And as they throw him to the ground, His breath comes in gasps. The hammer swings. Can you hear metal upon metal as the piercing takes place? They raise Him and with a jolt the cross has found its place.

Listen…

To the wagging heads, the heartless jeers, as He finally speaks, "Father, forgive them, they know not what they do." Taunting laughter, mournful wails. As blood flows down. He hears, He listens still, to the thief and gives hope of a final blessing, "This day you will be with me in Paradise." The crown roars, "Paradise, if you are the Christ, free yourself." Jesus pays them no mind. For his mind is on His mother. Looking into her soul he said, "Woman, behold your son" and looking at John, "behold your mother." Hear the time, the slow seconds ticking away the hours as he hung dying for you. As a gust of wind whipped sand, swirling about and the sky grew darker he cried in a loud voice, "My God, My God, why have you forsaken me?"

Listen…

To the wind whistling as he spoke softly almost longingly, "I thirst." Hear the bustle of the scoffers pushing the gall to His lips when His heart ached for righteousness. The wind is roaring now. The sky Is black as he looks to heaven saying with a gasp, "It is finished." Hear the crashing of the heavens, the ripping of the veil, as He breathed His last. Hear the lone centurion declare in amazement and in solemnity, "Surely this was the Son of

God." What do you hear? What silence holds your tongue as they lower him to the ground?

Listen...

To the fabric softly fall into place around His lifeless form. The men grunt and groan against the stone as it grinds against the ground to its place. Hear the wince of Mary as she walks, and the sword pierced her heart. Is your heart pierced too by all that you heard? Dig deep. Listen well to your heart when you ask yourself as Christ asked his disciples, "Who do you say I am?" May your response echo Peter's, "You are the Christ, the Son of the living God!" What say you? By some miracle, has your hearing too been restored?

Day 76
Cover up

Hidden in the darkness
We cover up our sin
We hide It where we think
The light won't enter in
We hold our precious treasure
While our secret's holding us
Back from true devotion
From the One who died for us.
We go through the motions
We serve, we sing, we pray.
While partial disobedience
Is leading to decay.
A faith that was on fire
A stumbling block did meet
A heart joyful to obey
Now timidly retreats
Slowly drifting on our own
Our pride holds us apart.
We somehow feel entitled
To keep this one sin in our heart.
Such lengths we go to cover up

The hole we've dug is deep.
We cling to what is broken
So we have no hands to reap.
But God is ever seeking us
And he knows our plight
He has sent the Spirit
To help us fight the fight.
He longs to lift our burdens
He lives to set us free
From sin that easily entangles
The outcome's up to you and me.
We always have a choice
It's not too late to change our mind
To sacrifice the sin
And leave it all behind.
We can walk in freedom
Christ can restore your soul
And heal the broken places
And create a saint that's whole.

Day 77
Poured Out

*But I Say to you that for every idle word men may
speak, they will give account of it in the day of judg-
ment. Matthew 12:36*

You punctured my vision, my hope
When you called me hopeless.
The repetitive shaking
Of my confidence in
Sharing an idea
Was my vision foolish to you?
Or couldn't your blindness
See my anticipation?
It's a habit of the heart
This finger pointing
This repetitive labeling
Of me as hopeless.
That word totally
Deflated my excitement.
Jabbing into my soul bringing
Recollection of the former
Times of former labels

Of times when I was accused
And accursed by similar words

Of personal degradation.
Sometimes I'm too weak
To believe that no child of God
Is hopeless in His eyes.
Surely this label cannot
Be nailed to my cross
By a brother
I try to erase the memory
But the wounding stains my soul
For this is not the first time
You've labeled me and liabled
Me before the Father
And my life's blood was poured
Upon the ground
The pain of the words spoken
Jarred me into silence
And halted for too long a time
Feelings that such a word would come
From lips that call for closeness
Hearing you say, "You're hopeless"
Separates my soul from you.
And even now after all of this
Do you feel remorse or justification?
Do you wag your head back and forth

At the cross of suffering your words Nailed me too?
Do you scoff at my pain?
Or do you stop to inhale my truth?

Day 78
The Clearing

As the battle rages deeper
In the heart where joy is found
Darkness seeks to find its places
In the light where joy abounds

Every ray of hope is clouded
By the rising of the flames
Fire threatens to consume us
Till we call on Jesus' name

Ashes cover like a cloak
Till the Spirit rises in us.
Sending winds to
Sweep away the smoke

In the clearing of the Spirit
We can sing a song of praise
For the Savior is our rescue
Darkness bows the knee to grace.

There is victory in each battle
When his joy fills up our soul
The prison walls are shattered
The love of Jesus makes us whole.

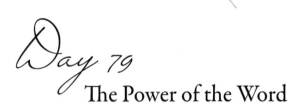

Day 79
The Power of the Word

Death and life are in the power of the tongue.
Proverbs 18:21

There are times when...
Words spoken
Are words lost when
No one is listening and
Meaning is tossed
Into the winds
There are times when...
Words can kill a soul
Anxious for solace
Emotions silently starve
Waiting for a morsel
Of kindness
Yet there are times when...
Words mend
Weaving strand and thread
Into a heart that once was dead
And then there are times when...
Words speak life

Into times of chaos
And of strife

Chose wisely just
What words you say
Speak kindly
With each breath

For there are times when...
Words bring life yet
There are times when...
Words bring death.

Day 80
The End of Our Faith

Before we were alive in the flesh
There was a vision by the Father.
We were known by him.
And He knew the price to be paid.
The ransom was precious
The separation from His Son.
Was His heart broken
As he tore his eyes away
From the eyes of His Son?
Oh, what price He paid for the glory.
Did the Spirit also minister to Him?
Did his final healing come
When salvation came to one soul?
Does His healing continue as
Souls he foreknew
Come to salvation?
Is our joy in Him His balm?
What soothed his spirit
At the daily suffering of his Son
The reviling, the naked laughter,
The jesting, the rejection of the Word?

How great the Father's love for us,
That he too would suffer for us
.The Father's heart was torn
Yet the Spirit whispered to Him
His own promise of mercy and
Peace on earth.
And glory shines upon Him
When he hears a hallelujah
From His throne
From a rejoicing soul
Who has received was revealed from the foundation.
The end of His faith.
The salvation of his soul.
And the Father is glorified again
And again as living stones
Lay one upon the other in unison
Resting on the chosen One.
The cornerstone and they
In submission raise a hallelujah to
The suffering Servant
Whose obedience and blood is the mortar
For His church that reaches out
In the Spirit to those chosen ones.
So they too may receive the end of

Their faith.
The salvation of their souls
This living hope born of the Father
Born on the cross

Is the fire in the heart of the faithful
So all may see the truth of the
Glory of the gospel of God?

Day 81
Still Before the Lord

We can't detect the origin of sound
At times it feels it is all around
A buzzing saw a blaring horn
Work on us until we're born

Weary heart and broken soul
Will in His yoke be made whole
Sorrow, chaos, all the noise
Stills beneath His gentle voice

Come to Him be set free
Peace for all eternity
Darkness yielding way to Light
Shed from His hands with glorious might

Hush! Now, let the roaring cease
In His grace find His peace
From the Word it's just the start
Of Godly love in the human heart

Mercy love and sorrow flowed
So we could such a great truth hold
We share with Him a mind renewed in
The blessing of this solitude

In silence sitting with the Son
All the pieces become one
What was missing has been found
When I sit with Him without a sound

He calls for you to come before
Him so your soul he can restore
And then His kingdom, it will come
When you sit quietly before the Son

"Solitude with God repairs the damage
done by the noise of the world"
Oswald Chambers

Day 82
Never Enough

"Let your conduct be without covetousness; be content with such things as you have "
Hebrews 13:5

O NE OF THE MOST OUTSTANDING moments of the 2017 film , The Greatest Showman, was when European Opera star Jenny Lind (played by Rebecca Ferguson) performed the song (sung by Loren Allred) Never Enough. What struck me was the mesmerizing power she gave to the words that 'set off a dream in me' and the implication that dream would have in her never being satisfied with the life she lived before the magic became real for her.

Isn't that how discontent begins? Something triggers us to believe a dream that doesn't belong to us? In Jenny's case she had her eye set on the dream of capturing the star of the show. It wasn't enough to be one of many stars she wanted Barnum. Anything less, would be well, never enough.

The song, the scenario, the struggle,-to have what is not ours-is the bane of the human race. We covet-run with hot envy–after something we don't have, desperate in our desire to possess the object of our dreams, thinking it will fulfill us ... that we become morally bankrupt. Incapable of being honest, trustworthy or truthful.

Eve faced it in the garden the insatiable appetite for what was off limits for her. One by one she threw off the cautious voice of God speaking softly for the capricious lies and coveted the apple that had set off a dream in her and she traded her never enough, her life with Adam as she knew it; her satisfaction of unity with God for the darkness of sin. Touching the apple didn't taint her, tasting it did– taking disobedience's cancer unto her pure mouth putrefied the dream of never enough. Too late to go back. No never again allowed.

We face it when we fail to be content with the garden God has placed us in. All it takes is a glance askew. A moment when the heart for God is asleep at the wheel and we're faced with a never enough enticement. Satan is swift and like a hunter will corner us with a temptation a mesmerizing urge to grasp the never enough brass ring. But we have the comfort and power of the Spirit to come to our aid and the sharp sword of the Word to echo a challenging NEVER to the "never enough" that taunt and tempt us.

Let us learn through the study of the Word and the fellowship of the Saints how to take captive every thought and learn to be content with our very lives so we came drown out that never enough voice as we listen to the all sufficient voice of our Savior who is ALWAYS enough.

Day 83
The Worth of our words

" So Samuel grew and the Lord was with him and (the Lord) let none of his words fall to the ground."
1st Samuel 3:19.

HAVE YOU EVER MET SOMEONE LIKE Samuel? Someone whose every word was significant, pregnant with meaning. Words you would ponder and query about; words that had meat on their bones. Words you were drawn to flesh out, try to give life and meaning to.

The words the prophet Samuel would speak were ones put into his mouth by the Lord-words with eternal significance and when Samuel spoke-people listened. They were mouth to ear words. Like the words of our Great Shepherd. His words, heart-life words would come from within to reverberate into the hearts and minds of His people.

Life-words are not to be wasted. They are like the precious drops of water to parched lips-not one drop is left to find its way into the sand. Words of warning, words of wisdom are meant to be absorbed into the tissue of your being, valued more than life itself

Consider the words of someone you have lost. Would you not give anything just to hold their words in your heart once more. This is how we should listen for life is fleeting and the voice of a loved one can be stilled so quickly by the winds of time. This flame that burns on the candle of our lives can quickly be swept away and burn no more. There is great worth in the utterance of the mouth. Learn to listen- let not one word fall to the ground to be grabbed up by the hungry grave.

Day 84
The Risk of Freedom

"... and everyone did what was right in their own eyes." Judges 17:6

FREEDOM, EVERYONE WANTS IT. THE ability to do what you want when you want. To be at your leisure to do what you want when you want. When we're little we want to grow up. When we grow up we want things to change. We're constantly on the lookout for that elusive moment of really being free.

But there's a big risk associated with freedom and that is accepting responsibility within limits. Without limits you would constantly be in debt, continuously be in need, and always in a state of wanting what you don't have...yet. Freedom comes with boundaries attached...freedom is a sort of prison minus the bars between you and the great big world outside that you can see but cannot touch. Some things are just off limits if you really wish to live contentedly.

The risk of freedom is that we want to stretch the rules until we break the rules. Then the walls of our ivory castle come crumbling down around us and we find that doing what seems right in our own eyes ends in lives lived in bankruptcy enslaved by our reckless actions.

The Israelites gained freedom from slavery and were given an overflowing land. They too had limits to live within. But they broke all the laws put in place by God until they found themselves enslaved to their human passions. They did what was right in their own eyes and turned order into chaos. They wound up being captured by a foreign nation with foreign gods. They had forsaken the God of their youth and again became slaves.

When will we stop? Becoming enslaved to our passions. Making ourselves victims of the circumstances we have created. When will we stop a bad habit that slips so seamlessly into bad lifestyle? Our decisions determine the course of our circumstances. Our course (or path) determines nature of our thinking. Our thinking determines the state of our freedom

If we desire to walk continuously in freedom we must remember to "Stand fast in the liberty by which Christ has made us free and do not be entangled with a yoke of bondage (Galatians 5:1). Stand firm refusing to do what is right in our own eyes but to do what is right in Gods eyes. So step my step, thought by thought hold tightly to your freedom and "Walk in the Spirit and you shall not fulfill the lusts of the flesh."(Galatians 5:16). For it is the hand of the flesh that can lead us astray, into enemy territory-into bondage.

"Look to Me, and be saved.." (Isaiah 45:22). Keep the eyes of your heart on the Lord and you will never again run the risk of crossing the line from freedom to bondage.

Day 85
Broken But Whole

" He heals the brokenhearted and binds up
their wounds."
Psalm 147:3

HOW MANY TIMES HAVE IN OUR LIVES have we broken something? Try as we may, our repair efforts usually leave some type of flaw in the original-a scar of sorts. Something breaks in our lives-whether it is self-imposed or because of the circumstances that mark and mar our very existence. These too are scars. Sometimes you can see them, but most scars remain hidden away in the dark crevices of our soul.

Soul scars are resilient. They break our hearts and, more often than not, prevent us from being the person God created us to be. Until they are excavated by a loving hand, they fester into fear, forlorn feelings, bitterness, and brokenness.

Scars can become our badge of 'honor' that we wield to like a shield in an effort to keep people at arm's length. This invisible shield keeps people from getting too close; but it also is our worst enemy–it becomes a wall to crouch behind- a crutch we lean into in an effort to self-protect.

I tucked myself behind my invisible shield, but it didn't protect me from glimpses of seeing my brother die when I was six; or keep the terror of being raped at the age of 10 from haunting and hunting me; it didn't take away the image of my father throwing a pitchfork into my 14-year-old brother's back, or lessen the load of guilt I felt for not being able to protect my mother from yet another beating. It didn't lighten the burden of shame I felt for years of my own sexual misconduct. But I held my shield anyway. It kept me in the shadows-kept me isolated. For 42 years I hid my brokenness in the shadow of that shield. I never realized that I kept myself in such darkness until the light of Jesus penetrated my self-protective device.

I was soul-sick, I was maimed when I met the mender of my broken and torn heart. I was convinced I was worthless until I learned I was worthy of His love. " ...the multitude marveled when they saw...the maimed made whole...the blind seeing, and they glorified the God of Israel." Matthew 15:31. The darkness I lived in blinded me and with the touch of the Master's hand, I could see. I was made whole. That day I surrendered my shield to Jesus and He loved all of me.

The beautiful thing about the love of Christ is that I began to be mended from the inside out. Images of the past slowly dissolved to become a mist that surely worked its way to the sea where all my sin and shame were cast. Forgiveness granted by my Savior keeps me from trying to go fishing for old memories. They are healed and my soul though it still bears the scars is healed and whole, mended by the Master.

I'm reminded of a lyric from a Bob Dylan* song that may strike a chord for you as you deal with any brokenness you may have: "... go to (Him) now, you can't refuse-when you ain't got nothing you've got nothing to lose....". So go to Jesus if you're broken, he is ever waiting to mend-even you. You too can be whole.

Day 86
Let There Be Light

I WAS COMING HOME IN WHAT HAD TO BE the darkest night of the year. You know the kind of dark that you can't see your hand in front of your face. It was one of those nights when the moon is fully hidden from view. I turned down our road and flipped on the bright lights on the car in order to see better. I was silently hoping the deer weren't out traveling on this moonless night.

I could see ahead the small light from the kitchen and the brighter light from the living room where I pictured my husband relaxing in front of the television. I was hoping he remembered I'd be home late and would have turned on the light that illuminates the walkway from the drive to the house. I was relieved as I put the car in park and turned off the engine and started my walk to the house. I walked in the darkness over the gravel driveway.

As soon as I put my foot on the cement the light came on. I breathed a sigh of relief as I walked to the door. I also thanked God who blessed me with a husband who remembered the small stuff. As I put my key in the door I could hear the commotion if the excited dogs behind the door. Bracing my self I unlocked the door to their happy whining and head butting. It was if they were saying "Yay mom's home and I need to be petted first."

That day I really appreciated the lights of home. It reminded me just how important light is to us humans. God knew how important it was. It was the first thing he created after creating the heavens and the earth .

The first words spoken by God were: "Let there be light" God saw the light, that it was good…" Genesis 1:3. From the very beginning God saw that it was good to have light.

Very early in the ministry of Jesus, Jesus also pointed to the goodness of light, giving it an added distinction of being in the very nature of His followers by saying : ". You are the light of the world (Matthew 5:14)

With that light , you have a responsibility: you must as Jesus says: "Let your light so shine that all men might see your good works and glorify your Father in heaven." Matthew 5:16

We are to have a 'transfigurative' effect with the light that is in us. So that like a city on a hill, the glow of our light points others to the Holy.

Sometimes it takes a power outage that sends us running for candles and flashlights; sometimes it takes a moonless night for us to really appreciate the goodness of light. Other times it takes the diligent work of a believer to shine the light of God's goodness when a friend is at the end of their rope; the sending of a thoughtful card in the mail ;the calming heart of a pastor of a small church at a hospital beside;or the simple friendly greeting to a stranger—the light of you, can change the course of a life-so let there be light. And let the glory of God shine through.

About the Author

PRISCELLA LEWIS IS KNOWN BY HUN-dreds of people for her pickles. Before settling down to marriage with children, she ran a business with her family called Priscella's Homestyle Products. She is a very active and involved member of a mid-sized church in Rootstown Ohio, helping with cooking, food pantry, gardening, and other ministries of the church.

Although she has been writing in journals for most of her 72 years, this is her first book. Priscella is an active hiker; enjoys canning, gardening and food preparation. Her and her husband, Bob, have raised two children, Chris and Rebecca who have blessed their lives thus far, with 3 grandchildren.

Priscella has a farmer's heart. She grew up on a 73 acre farm in rural Ohio. She is the third oldest of her parents' 8 children.